Making
Shaker Furniture

Making
Shaker Furniture

Barry Jackson

Guild of Master Craftsman Publications

First published 1990 by Guild of Master Craftsman
Publications Ltd, Castle Place, 166 High Street,
Lewes, East Sussex BN7 1XU

Colour and cover photography
by Philip McCarthy

ISBN 0 946819 22 X

Designed by Robert and Jean Wheeler Design Associates

Printed in Great Britain by Grosvenor Press (Portsmouth) Ltd

Contents

Acknowledgements

Making Shaker Furniture has been a learning experience for me, and I thank my patron, Alan Phillips and his staff for making this possible.

Together with all students of Shaker culture, I am indebted to Faith and Edward Deming Andrews and the various American institutions who have promoted a greater public awareness of this subject.

I would like to thank the many people who freely gave help and encouragement during the two years it took to produce the material for this book. I am also grateful for the kind assistance of Judith Elsdon, assistant curator of the American Museum, Bath; and David Cole for photography.

I extend personal thanks to my two friends Graham Bacon and John Wilson who unselfishly provided essential materials when most needed. Finally, I thank my wife, Merry, for sustenance throughout this project.

In a book which spans over 200 years of history, I have had to rely on many sources other than my own first hand observations. Those books which I found of particular help are listed on page 126, both by way of acknowledgement to their authors and as a recommendation for further reading.

Foreword

On visiting the Barclay Gallery, Brighton, some three years ago, I was immediately attracted to several turned bowls, which as well as having a most ingenious and attractive wave form pattern, were aesthetically pleasing and meticulously finished. Further examples appeared in Bristol, Glasgow and the Design Centre, London. All were by the same man – Barry Jackson – but no one could offer a satisfactory explanation of how he achieved their unique laminated construction.

When I contacted Barry to find out more, I was further intrigued to learn that he also made authentic copies of Shaker furniture. The Shakers and their work have fascinated me for over thirty years and if I get to America one day, then the main attraction will be to see their furniture, artefacts and remaining buildings. Sadly, apart from the American Museum at Bath, there is little of their work to be seen in this country.

When Barry supplied some impeccable drawings to show his bowl construction, I realised that with his superb craftsmanship and knowledge of Shaker work, he might be persuaded to produce Shaker furniture projects. He agreed readily and the projects began to emerge. All were comprehensively illustrated and photographed complete with text which required no editing, and the accompanying pieces proved Barry's excellence as a craftsman.

Woodworkers following published plans are often let down by authors who have overlooked vital components or dimensions. But fourteen years as an engineer, followed by a further twelve in charge of a school craft department, have ensured that Barry thinks of everything that will make his projects a success – after all, he has been producing them for some years. And as you will discover, each project has been completed in entirety to provide the excellent photographs that complement the drawings, cutting lists and clear instructions.

Like Barry, my first introduction to the work of the Shaker communities came through the classic volumes by Faith and Edward Deming Andrews. We have this husband and wife team to thank for a lifetime devoted to collecting and researching the work of the Shakers. As the Andrews' pioneering work commenced over sixty years ago, there were still a few surviving Shakers who were able to provide authentic and detailed background information, and subsequent writers are all indebted to their earlier researches.

Through the projects in this book, Barry and I hope that you will become equally appreciative of the Shakers. We both agree that we too would have enjoyed working in their communities – although we could not have accepted their insistence on celibacy! The Shaker communities would certainly have welcomed Barry Jackson into their midst, for he possesses all their qualities – superb craftsmanship, innovative and design skills, and the ability to communicate.

John Haywood Stoke Abbott August 1990

Introduction

The Shakers are members of a communal religious sect which flourished in America during the nineteenth century. By embracing the basic principles of purity, simplicity and unity, they created a unique culture whose importance is now universally recognised. As these principles were absorbed into their lives, the Shakers developed an unusually high degree of craftsmanship and at the same time a distinctly individual style of furniture.

I have prepared material for a selection of projects which will enable both reader and maker alike to learn more about these extraordinary people and their work. Each piece has been faithfully reproduced from museum measured drawings of original examples made mainly between 1820 and 1860 when the quality and style of furniture was at its finest.

In recreating these pieces, the home craftsman will, like myself, discover the subtle qualities of Shaker charm.

History of the Shakers

The Shaker sect is one of America's earliest communal utopian societies, which still survives today, albeit with just a handful of Believers. Although officially titled 'The United Society of Believers in Christ's Second Appearance', they became more commonly known as Shakers because of their ecstatic dancing when holding religious services.

Whether man, woman or child, each member would be taught to accept the doctrines of communalism, celibacy and both racial and sexual equality. Devotion to these principles, combined with the pursuit of spiritual perfection, resulted in the creation of a unique culture which has endured for over 200 years.

The Shaker faith was taken to the New World by an English woman named Ann Lee and a small group of followers. Prompted by a vision and sustained by the conviction that 'Christ in his Second Appearance' was within them, they sailed from Liverpool, landing in New York in 1774.

Before Mother Ann's death ten years later, despite persecution and mob violence, seeds of the Shaker faith had been planted in upper New York State, Massachusetts, Connecticut, New Hampshire and Maine. The next decade saw the organisation of twelve communities and the establishment of a central church at New Lebanon, New York.

During this formative period, converts were drawn almost entirely from local country folk. They brought with them energy and vitality together with the simple customs and rural craft traditions of colonial New England and the upper Hudson river. These formed the basic ingredients that were to play an essential part in the development of a unique American culture and its corresponding craftsmanship.

At the beginning of the nineteenth century, with a membership of 1000, the Shaker faith was firmly established. By 1820 it had extended into Ohio, Kentucky and Indiana, bringing the total number of communities to eighteen.

The belief in purity, simplicity and unity which permeated all aspects of the Believers' lives had by this time filtered through into the workshops. Craftsmanship reached an uncommon level of excellence and a distinctly individual character came to life in the Shakers' work.

As the movement flourished, attempts at self-sufficiency resulted in an incredible growth of industrial and agricultural activity. Production soon became so great as to satisfy not only their own needs but also those of a 'worldly' market. The resulting wealth enabled the Shakers to invest in extensive areas of farming land and forestry which were rich in materials to feed their rapidly growing industries.

Between 1850 and 1860 the number of Believers had risen to a maximum of 6000, owning around 50 000 acres with over 1000 well-equipped shops, farm buildings and dwellings. At this time, however, social and economic changes were taking place in America that were ultimately to cause the decline of the United Society. Although the doctrine of celibacy did not help their survival, the effects of the Industrial Revolution and the Civil War were the main causes.

Disintegration started before the end of the Civil War and numbers began to fall drastically. The recorded population in 1875 was 2500, decreasing to 1000 by 1900. As the downward trend continued into our own century, communities closed, properties were sold, and craft industries became limited to a minimal production of oval boxes and chairs. By 1960 all the remaining members had been transferred to the two last surviving communities at Canterbury, New Hampshire and Sabbathday Lake, Maine.

These are primarily living museums, but the seeds of the faith remain alive in the seven elderly Shaker sisters who still live there, the last True Believers. As directed by the Ministry, the Shaker Covenant was officially closed in 1957.

The everyday life of the Shakers was highly regulated and industrious. Each day passed according to a set pattern, with order and precision apparent in their work. All was dedicated to the pursuit of excellence, absolute simplicity and utility. The culmination of these principles resulted in a rare and timeless beauty of enduring inspiration to succeeding generations. ■

Sewing Stand

This sewing stand, with its pure simple lines, is one example from the many square-topped pedestal tables made for the Sisters' workshops.
The two drawers can be used from both sides. This device, which enabled two sewers to work together, combines function with economy of space, two characteristics typical of Shaker thought.

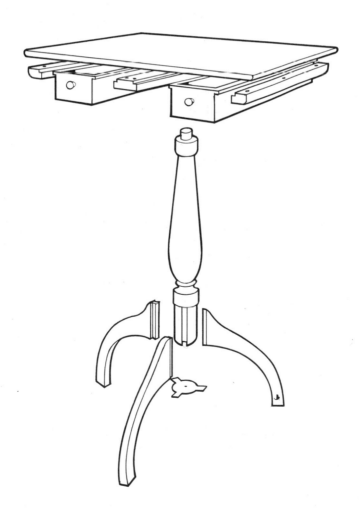

MAPLE AND CHERRY were commonly used, the tops and drawers sometimes made in pine. Finishes varied from painting a dark red to staining light brown and varnishing. I have used North American rock maple finished with a transparent sealer followed by wax polish.

A certain amount of ingenuity, patience and skill will be required to produce this stand. It should prove an interesting challenge to the more experienced woodworker.

Top

Arrange the boards to give the most interesting effect, making sure that the annular rings alternate as shown in Fig 1. This will ensure greater stability.

It is essential to form good butt joints; shoot the edges with great care then mark out for dowelling. The dowels will strengthen the joints, improve location and make gluing easier.

Position the 6mm diameter holes 50mm from each end and one in the centre. Drill the holes 15mm deep. This allows a slight clearance for each of the 28mm long dowels.

Of the many adhesives available, I prefer a powdered resin wood glue. The inconvenience of having to mix it with water is compensated for by its reliability. Glue the top using two sash cramps with a weight placed on the centre of the middle board to maintain flatness. Allow approximately six hours setting time before planing down to the finished thickness of 14mm, then round off the edges and finish sanding.

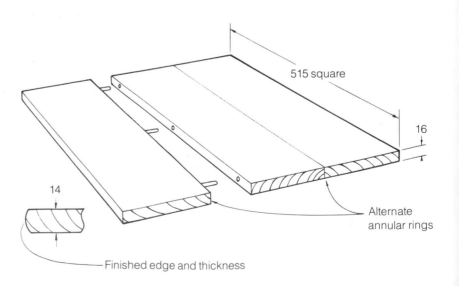

515 square

16

14

Alternate annular rings

Finished edge and thickness

Fig 1 Top assembly

Drawers

Rebate the edges of the drawer fronts, then cut the grooves which accommodate the bottoms. A dry assembly is advisable, checking that all is square and the bottoms fit easily in the grooves. Before gluing and cramping, drill the holes for the knobs 8mm diameter by 11mm deep. When the drawer assembly has dried, the slides can be glued and pinned, taking care that the top, sides and ends are flush. Originally, drawer and column/leg joints were dovetailed by hand. Modern-day adhesives, however, enable less time-consuming methods to be used without sacrificing strength.

Fig 2 Pinning the drawer slides

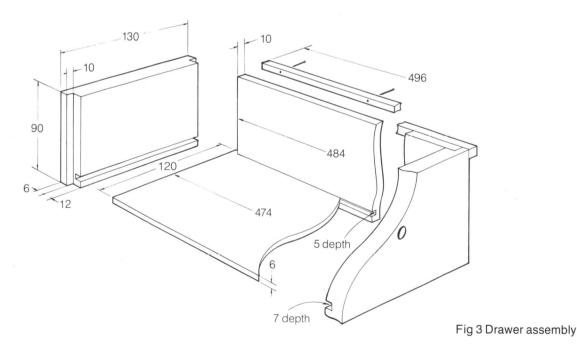

Fig 3 Drawer assembly

Fig 4 Gluing and cramping the drawers

Fig 5 Rebating the supports

Drawer supports

Check that the supports are flat, parallel and square to each other before rebating. When the rebates have been cut the bottom outer sides of the side supports can be rounded off. Mark out the position of the screw holes, then drill with a 5mm bit and countersink. A 25mm diameter flat bit is used to drill the column spigot hole. Place the drawers and supports in position on the underside of the table top at right angles to the direction of the boards. Leave a 1mm gap between each for clearance and bradawl through the screw holes. The supports and drawers can now be sanded, paying particular attention to the rebates and slides. Slight clearance in the screw holes will allow for final adjustment between drawer and support when screwing down.

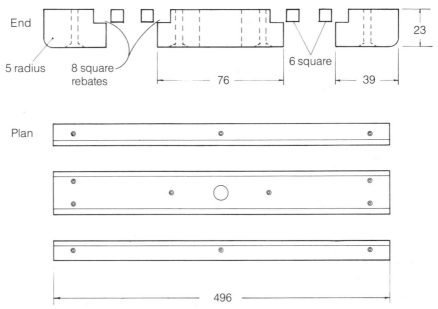

End

5 radius   8 square
            rebates

6 square

23

76   39

Plan

496

Fig 6 Drawer supports and slides

Fig 7 Assembling the supports with drawers in position

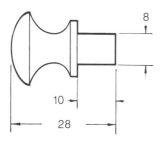

Fig 8 Dimensions of the knobs

Drawer knobs

Offcuts from the drawer supports provide the material for the four knobs. Two 80mm lengths are rough turned between centres, then held in a chuck to shape the peg ends first, using a pre-drilled piece of scrapwood to check for fit. The waist is cut, sanded and parted off to length. Holding the peg end in the chuck, each head can be rounded off and sanded. The pegs are now ready for gluing to the drawers.

Fig 9 Parting off drawer knobs to length

Fig 10 Rounding off drawer knob head

Column

The method described here, of jointing the legs to the column, is one which I devised for mass producing. Hand cut sliding dovetails were originally used, as described in Pedestal Tables, page 102.

Using Fig 11 as your guide, turn the column between centres leaving approximately 1mm on the diameters for final finishing. The section at the base, to be mortised, is taken to finished size and great care must be taken to maintain a flat parallel profile.

Fig 11 Column and legs to scale

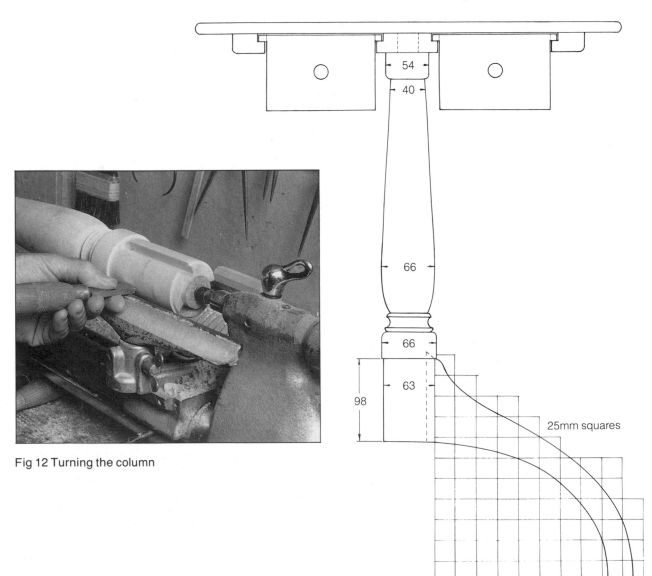

Fig 12 Turning the column

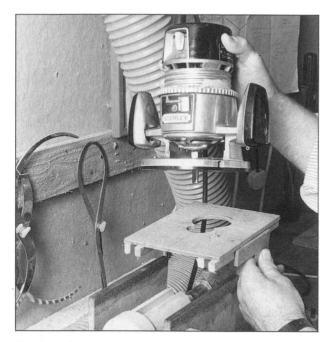

Fig 13 The box-type mortising fixture

Fig 14 Routing the mortise

The driving centre is now replaced by a three-jaw chuck. This adds more stability to the column when cutting the mortises. No doubt the primitive-looking fixture I have made to do this will amuse many, but I have found it to be very effective and accurate. If the expense can be justified, there are very probably alternative fixtures available on the market to do this operation.

The reinforced box-type structure shown in Figs 13 and 14 is made entirely from scrap pieces of wood, the inner sides centralised and made parallel to the lathe bed, then clamped to the bench. The upper edges of these sides act as guides for the slide arrangement which is screwed to the router base.

The slide fit must be sufficiently tight to avoid any vibration when cutting the mortises. To control the extent of travel, a stop is pinned to the outer side of the slide and locates on the reinforced section of the box base when the router is at the end of its cut. Using the dividing head, the three mortise positions can be determined and secured for each cut. A 12.7mm diameter two-fluted straight cutter is ideal for this purpose.

Before starting each cut, check that both ends of the column are secure and the dividing head is firmly locked in position. To minimise strain, the required depth of 12.5mm is best achieved by taking about three cuts. When this is done, finish the angled part of each mortise with a mallet and chisel (Fig 15). The column can now be finished off between centres and left on the lathe for dry fitting of the leg tenons.

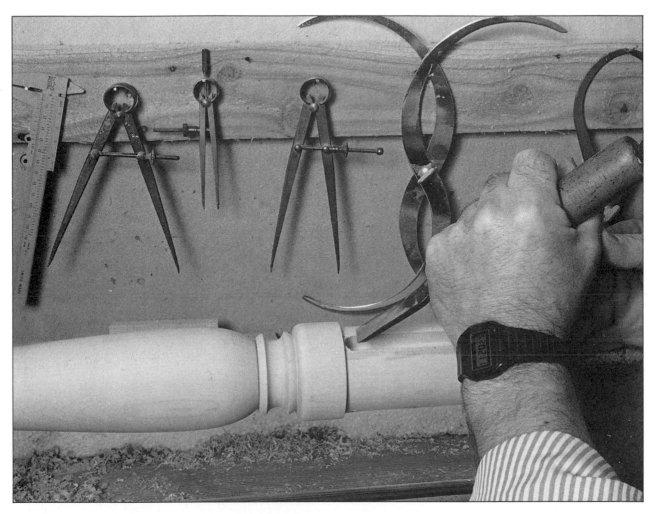

On lathes which do not have a dividing head, an alternative method of locking the column in the required positions will have to be devised.

One suggestion would be to cut out a disc from 9mm plywood with the centres of each mortise position marked out radially from centre to the rim, which must just clear the lathe bench when centred and screwed to the outboard faceplate.

If there is no outboard turning facility the rim of the disc will have to clear the lathe bed when centred and screwed to the inboard faceplate. It will also be necessary to hold the column between centres when mortising and to drill a clearance hole for the drive centre in the ply disc. A pointer taped securely to the headstock rests on the rim and corresponds with each mark on the disc rim when the column is rotated. A block of wood, locating on the face of the disc, can be secured to the lathe bench, then clamped to the disc in each of the three positions.

Fig 15 Finishing the angled part of the mortise by hand

Legs

On a piece of card, draw and cut out a full-size template of the legs. Mark out the legs as shown in Fig 16 and cut the flat side of the tenon only. Sand this flat side dead straight and square. Clamp each leg to the bench and cut the tenons. I have used a power router with a dovetail cutter which gives the required shoulder angle to match the column (Fig 17). When all the tenons have been cut and fit well, re-mark the angled projection at the head of each tenon and saw the complete profile. Finish sanding the legs, then dry fit into the column-base mortises, making any necessary adjustments before gluing.

Fig 16 Marking out the legs, overlapping with the template

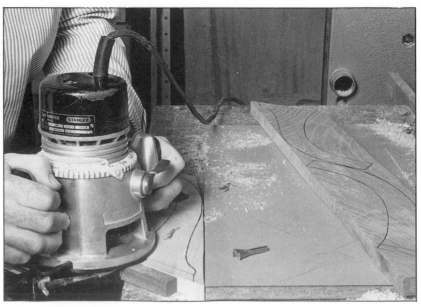

Fig 17 Routing the leg tenons

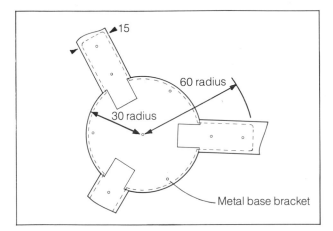

Fig 18 The metal base bracket

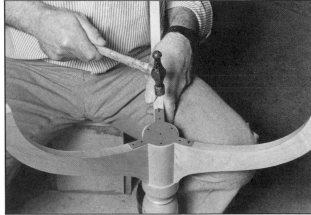

Fig 19 Pinning the base bracket

Base bracket

Mark out the base bracket as shown by dotted lines in Fig 18. Lightly centre-pop the pin positions then drill with a 1mm diameter bit. Cut out the shape with tin-snips and file or grind the edges smooth. Using gimp pins, pin the bracket to the column base and legs.

Assembly and finishing

The column spigot can now be glued to the centre support, taking care to determine the correct position of legs in relation to the top. When the glue has set, seal the complete stand, then wax polish to a high gloss finish. Clear gloss varnish could be used as an alternative. For the final touch, a little extra polish or candlewax is applied to the slides to improve movement of the drawers. ■

CUTTING LIST
Finished sizes in mm

Rock Maple

		Length	Width	Thickness	
	Top	515	515	16	A
2	Side supports	496	39	23	
1	Central support	496	76	23	B
4	Drawer fronts	130	90	18	
4	Drawer sides	484	90	10	
2	Drawer bottoms	474	120	6	C
4	Drawer slides	496 ·	6	6	
3	Legs	380	100	18	D
	Column	490	67 dia.		E
	Base bracket (sheet steel)	120	120	1	
10	Gimp pins	12.5			
18	1½in Number 8 Countersunk-head screws				

A The number of pieces used for the top will depend on the width of boards available. I have used three pieces cut from 178mm wide boards prepared to 16mm thickness, allowing for finish planing to 14mm thickness after gluing.

B Add an extra 80mm length to the central support for the drawer knobs.

C Plywood can be used as an alternative for the drawer bases.

D It is possible to economise on the length of board used for the legs by overlapping with the template when marking out.

E Allow up to 10mm extra on diameter for roughing out.

Oval Boxes

The Shakers produced their first oval boxes and carriers in the 1790s and continued to do so, with very little change in design, until Brother Delmer Wilson completed the last set of carriers in 1955 at the Sabbathday Lake Community, Maine, thus bringing to an end one of the most successful Shaker craft industries.

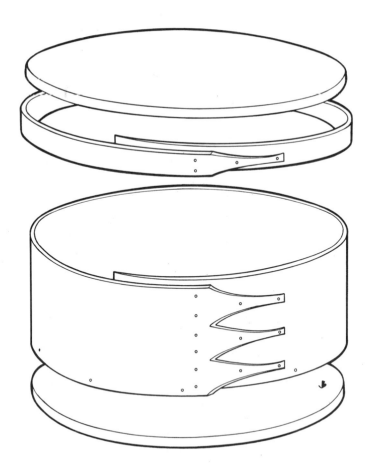

T HEY WERE MADE originally, for the Shakers' own use, in nests of up to twelve graduated sizes to hold all manner of domestic goods other than liquids. Proving to be extremely popular because of their novelty and usefulness, large quantities were manufactured for sale to the 'outside world', where the Shakers soon gained a reputation for honesty and excellent craftsmanship.

Some of the boxes, known as carriers, were fitted with folding loop handles. On others, without lids, the handle was fixed. All shared the same distinctive feature of 'swallow tails' delicately cut into the overlapping sides. Broad thin bands of maple, cherry, birch or oak were used for the oval – and sometimes round – sides, pine for the bottom and top inserts.

I have made three oval boxes using cherry and pine, each providing an interesting exercise involving several aspects of woodworking. The methods described will give the best results and are most suitable when making small numbers. For those wishing to produce larger quantities some time-saving suggestions have been included under the heading Production Methods.

Tacks and pins

My search for the correct sizes of copper tacks to secure the box sides was absolutely fruitless until, while measuring up the Drop Leaf Table (see page 89) at the American Museum, Bath, I mentioned this to the Assistant Curator Judith Elsdon. She helpfully suggested that I contact John Wilson, one of the most prominent makers of and lecturers on Shaker boxes in the United States.

An immediate response included the following information: copper tacks @ $3 per 1oz pack, plus air mail postage @ $3 for up to 4 packs.

Sizes: * 2 for Box 1, * 1½ for Box 2, * 1 for Box 3, and size Long. A 1oz pack of size 1 is sufficient for 30 to 40 of the smallest Box 3.

See Sources and Suppliers, page 126, for further details.

Copper pins, which were used to secure the side bands to the oval insets, are to our knowledge no longer made. A 10mm length pin sawn from the sharp end of a hardwood toothpick is a practical and attractive substitute, or alternatively copper tacks, size Long.

I have since had the pleasure of being host to John during a lecture/demonstration tour of the UK. Some of his tips have been included under Production Methods, page 35, and I am confident that anyone fortunate enough to attend any of his workshops is in for an enjoyable treat.

Moulds

Each mould can be made either in a single piece from solid timber, or in several layers of either blockboard or plywood offcuts at least 25mm thick. Lamination is the more practical and economical method to use in most home workshops with equipment of limited size.

From the plan (Fig 2) make a full-size template and mark out the shape of sufficient layers to exceed the depth of the box sides by approximately 20mm. These can be cut out by bandsaw and sanded accurately to the line on the disc sander. Check that all the sides are flush when laid on top of each other then, using a sharp knife, score lines on the surfaces to be glued. This will provide a better key and help prevent the pieces from sliding out of position when gluing.

Before assembling, two holes are drilled and countersunk through the top surface of the bottom layer to accommodate screws which secure a spigot to the base. The projecting spigot, sawn from a length of 50mm square scrapwood, enables the completed mould to be held securely in the vice when in use.

Fig 1 The two larger moulds in laminated ply, the smallest has been cut from one piece of solid timber

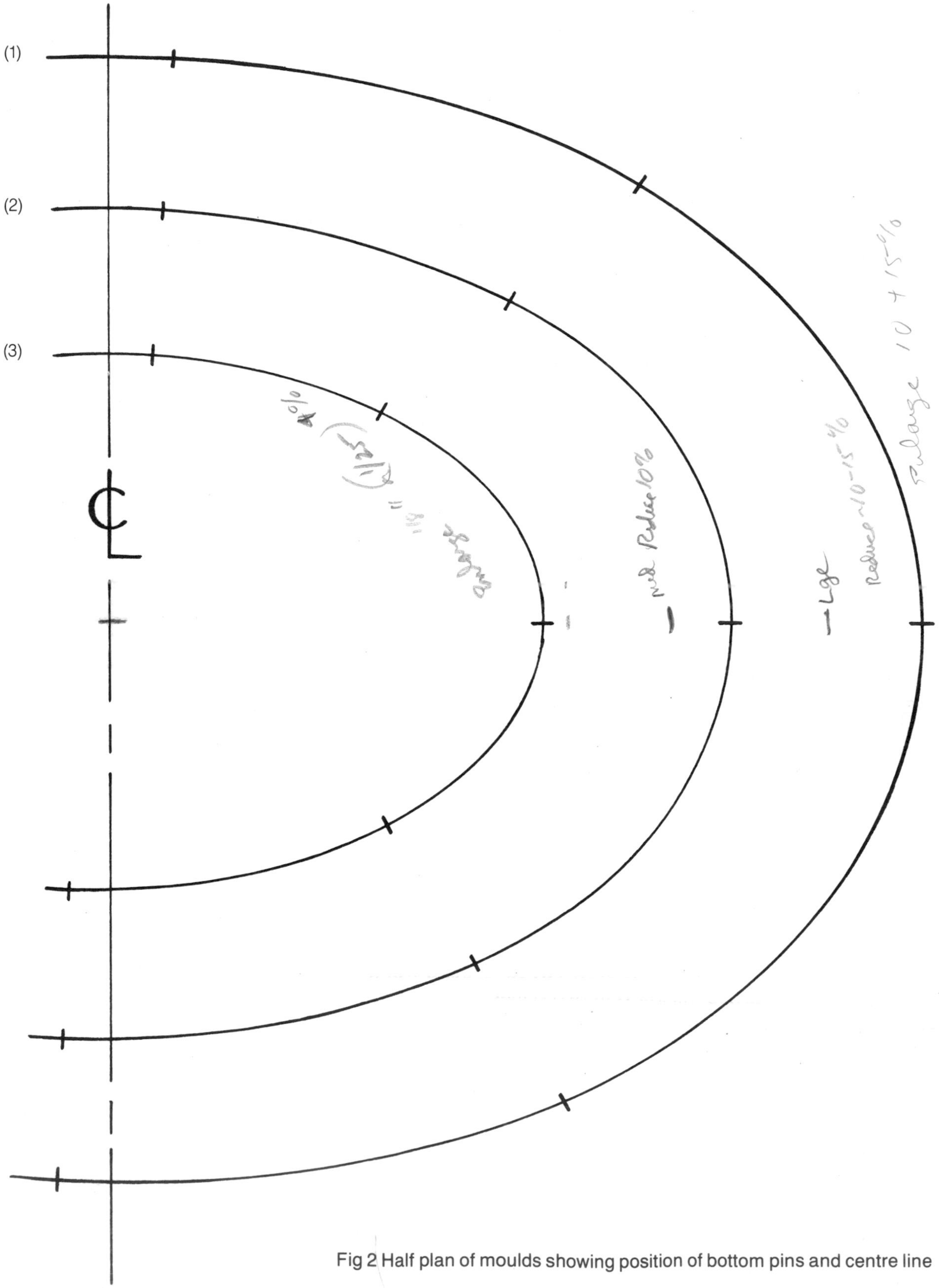

(1)

(2)

(3)

Ͼ L

angle 1½" (6¼) A%

nvd Reduce 10%

~Lge
Reduce ~10~15%

enlarge 10 + 15%

Fig 2 Half plan of moulds showing position of bottom pins and centre line

Glue and screw the spigot to the underside of the bottom layer, then glue and cramp all the layers together checking again that all sides are flush. When the glue has set, clean up the sides and mark the centre line on the top surface of the mould.

Tacking fixture

To ease the tacking operation, a fixture can be quickly made using a 200mm length of 30 to 50mm diameter heavy duty steel tube, a piece of scrapwood 50×100×180mm long, and two bolts with nuts. Cut a 'V' groove in the scrap block then, holding the tube firmly in the position shown in Fig 3, drill both bolt holes through the tube and block.

Counterdrill the underside of the block to accommodate each bolt head, feed the bolts from the bottom and tighten the nuts with a spanner.

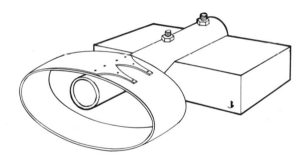

Fig 3 Tacking fixture

Side band

Starting with a board of sufficient length, prepared to the required width, bandsaw a thin strip for the box side. The sawn band will need to be hand planed to finished thickness in two stages.

First, clamp the end of the band to a flat bench then plane away from the clamp. Second, re-position the clamp farther up the band at as short a distance as is necessary to allow for planing the remaining area towards the clamp. This second stage must be done very carefully with the blade set for a fine cut otherwise the band will concertina.

Using abrasive paper, round off one long edge which will eventually be the top rim of the box side. With the appropriate full-size drawing as a guide (Figs 4, 5 or 6), make a template to mark out the swallow tails and position of tack holes.

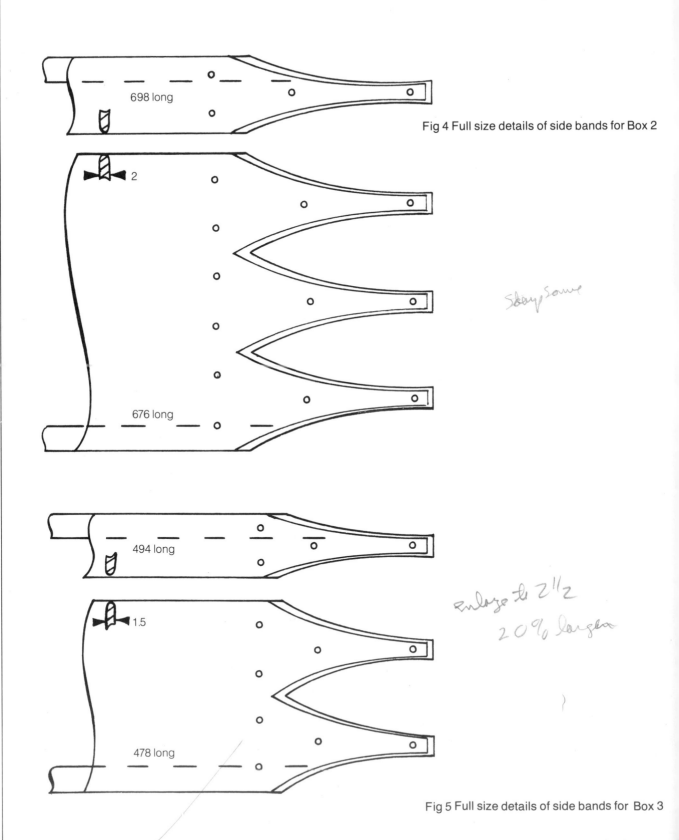

Fig 4 Full size details of side bands for Box 2

698 long

676 long

2

stay same

494 long

478 long

1.5

enlarge to 2½
20% larger

Fig 5 Full size details of side bands for Box 3

Reduce to
3 1/2"
Enlarge to 5 1/8

Fig 6 Full size details of side bands for Box 1

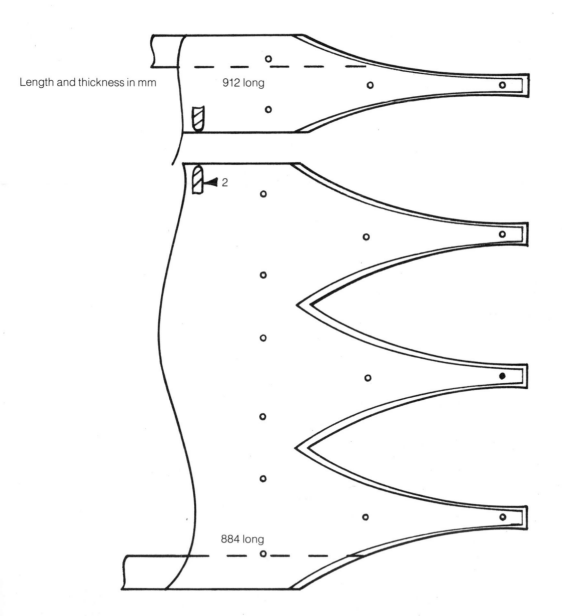

Length and thickness in mm   912 long

◄ 2

884 long

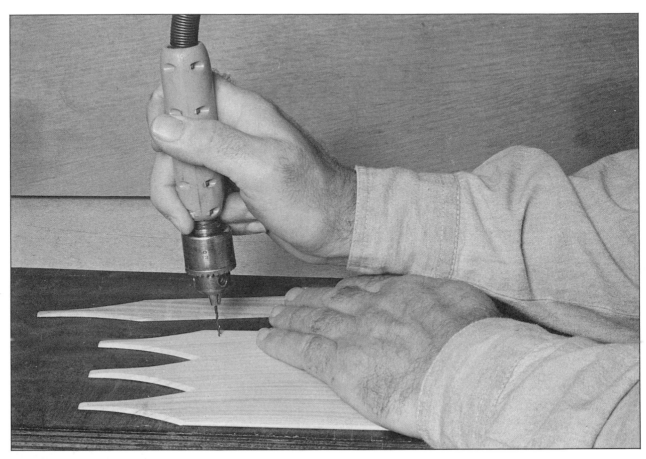

Fig 7 Pre-drilling the tack holes

Fig 8 Cutting the swallow tail shapes

Fig 9 Take care when cutting the chamfers

Sewing stand

Oval boxes

Hancock bench

Peg rails and knobs with a looking glass and candlesconce hanging from them

The looking glasses with the peg rail in the foreground

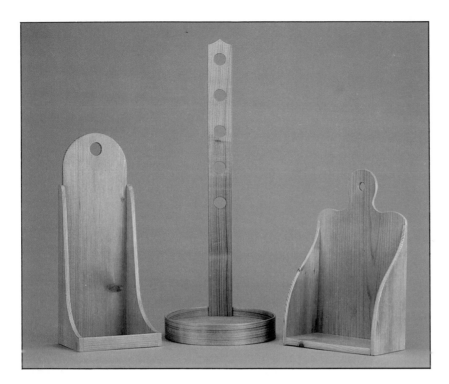

Hanging candlesconces

Adjustable candlesconce

Drying stands

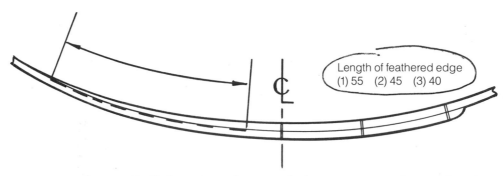

Length of feathered edge
(1) 55   (2) 45   (3) 40

Fig 10 Plan view of overlap

Drill these 1mm diameter holes next (Fig 7), then with a sharp blade and plenty of care, cut out the shape of the tails (Fig 8) before chamfering (Fig 9). To protect the band and bench surface during this operation, lay a piece of flat scrapwood above and below the band when clamping to the bench.

Slightly round off the end of each tail with abrasive paper, then cut the band to length at the opposite end and plane or sand to a feather edge, see Fig 10.

The band can now be immersed in a bath of hot water and left to soak for about two hours, topping up occasionally with more hot water to maintain temperature.

Cut a length of cord or strong string long enough to wrap round the mould five or six times. Make a noose at one end, then put to one side of the mould which should now be fastened securely in a vice.

Remove the soaked band from the bath and wrap tightly round the mould, positioning the vertical line of pre-drilled tack holes to correspond with the centre line marked on top of the mould. Loop the noose round the band and tighten before binding and fastening the remaining cord. Tension ought to be just sufficient to allow the insertion of thin spacers as shown in Fig 11. These prevent impressions being made by the string on the soft wet band.

Fig 11 The bound, soaked band with protective inserts

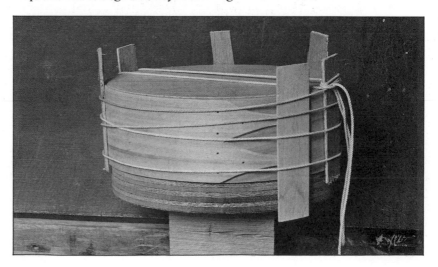

Check that the tail ends are well held down and leave for several days. When completely dry, mark the band at each tail end and then remove the cord and now-oval box side. Sand the inner and outer sides smooth but do not remove the tail-end location marks.

Clamp the tacking fixture (Fig 3) to a bench then, holding the band firmly, with tails in position, rest it on the steel tube and tack the sides, starting with the two middle tack holes in the centre line row. Repeat with the remaining holes, taking extra care not to split the tail ends which are done last.

Mark out and drill push-fit clearance holes (Fig 12) for the tacks or pins which will secure the sides to the oval inserts.

Fig 12 Drilling the base insert tack or pin holes

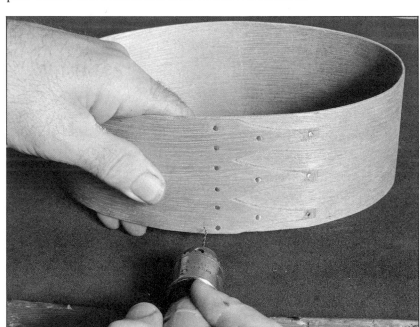

Fig 13 Tacking the base insert

Oval inserts

The oval top and bottom inserts are made from pine board prepared to the required thickness: (1) 8.5mm, (2) 6.5mm, (3) 6.5mm. Place the inverted mould on to the board and mark out the oval bottom. Bandsaw roughly to shape, then disc sand slightly outside the line to provide a tight fit inside the box base.

Press into position and, if using copper tacks size Long, tack the sides (Fig 13). If using the wooden pins, the holes will need to be drilled slightly deeper to a depth of 7mm before tapping well in and sanding flush to the sides.

Lids

The same procedure is repeated when making the lid, but with a mould 40mm thick which has been marked out using the outside edge of the finished box base as a template.

Finish

When the Shakers used paint on their boxes instead of varnish, the greens, yellows, blues and ruddy browns were occasionally thinned, sometimes until almost a transparent stain. Later examples were varnished over a light stain then polished. I have chosen to varnish the bare wood before finishing with wax polish.

Production methods

If large quantities of boxes are to be produced, the time taken to prepare the side bands will have to be reduced. Although more expensive, the ideal solution is to arrange a supply of already prepared bands with your wood dealer. A point worth noting is that if the thin bands are cut by circular saw, they are more inclined to bow than when cut with a bandsaw.

The tails have to be chamfered individually but the initial shapes could be bandsawn in clamped sets of, say, six bands at a time. The tack holes can also be drilled in sets.

It is not essential to tie the soaked bands on the moulds and leave until dry before tacking. The soaked band need only be wrapped tightly round the mould momentarily while marking the position of the tail ends, followed immediately by tacking the sides, inserting the oval bases and pinning.

With practice these operations only take a few minutes, and if repeated with small batches of bands soaking at the same time, several boxes can be assembled in an hour.

This method has an enormous time-saving advantage over the one previously described, but as the wet bands dry and shrink on the bases, slight distortion of the oval-shaped top rim can occur and, at the worst, albeit rarely, the box sides can split. However, when producing in large quantities, a small percentage of loss has to be allowed for. ■

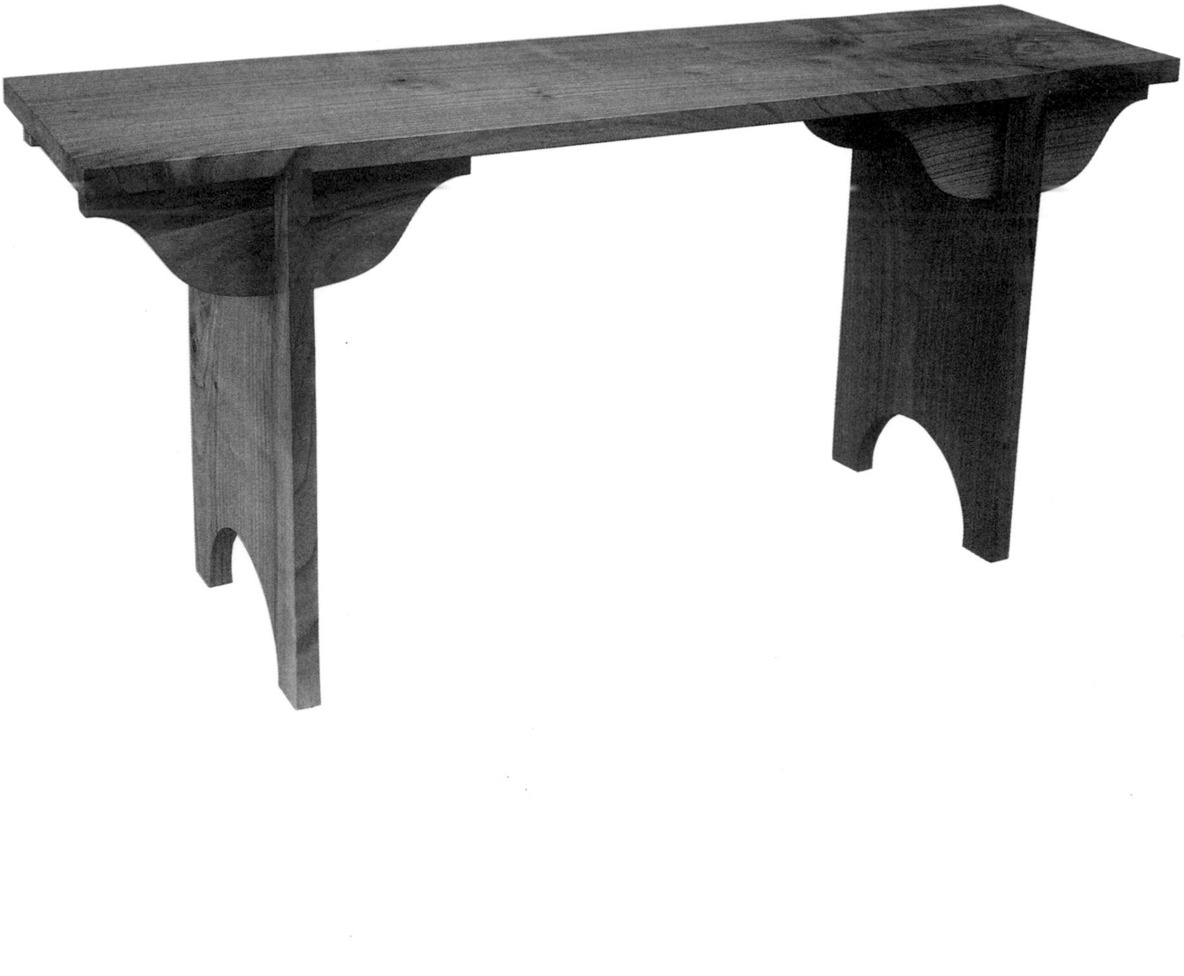

Hancock Bench

This small bench seat has been made in cherry
using measurements taken from an original
example at the Hancock Shaker Village,
Massachusetts. Also at Hancock is a longer pine
bench, with very similar butterfly-wing brackets.
Construction is identical, but for the addition of a
back rest. In the dining rooms and meeting houses
of some communities, these were eventually
replaced by the more comfortable slat-back chairs.

Preparation

Board prepared to 19mm thickness is used for all the pieces. Cut these to the required sizes, then lightly hand plane or sand the surfaces smooth, ensuring that all is square and straight. Smoothing the pieces at this stage will improve accuracy when marking out and jointing, although more care must be given to protecting the surfaces during these operations.

Brackets

A template, as shown in Fig 1 and drawn in 25mm squares, is cut from thin card and used to mark out the brackets. Saw the profiles and joints, remembering to leave sufficient material for cleaning up to the lines. A chisel is used for cleaning up the joints and, ideally, a drum sander for the curved profiles. Centres for the 5mm diameter screw holes are now marked out, drilled and countersunk.

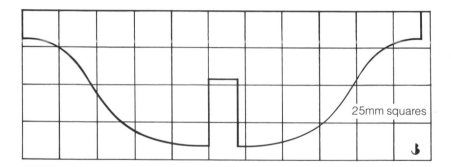

25mm squares

Fig 1 Template for brackets

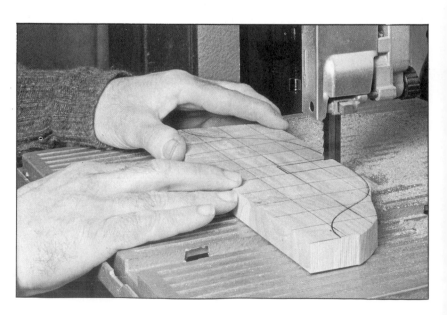

Fig 2 Bandsawing the bracket joints

Legs

Mark out the leg joints 25mm in from the sides, 50mm deep, then saw and finish off as for the bracket joints (Fig 3). These can now be checked for fit and, if necessary, adjusted to offer some resistance without being too tight. The 80mm radius semicircles are marked out next, then sawn and sanded smooth to the line. Again, a drum sander would be very useful for this purpose.

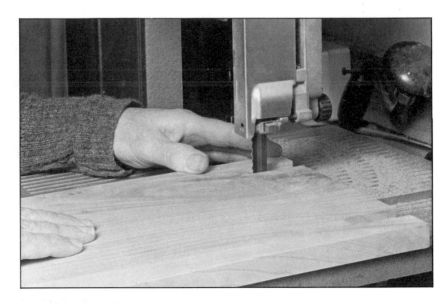

Fig 3 Bandsawing the leg joints, remembering to leave enough material for cleaning up

Seat

Use the more attractively figured face of the board for the top side of the seat and mark out the 3mm deep grooves for the legs on the underside. To cut these I have used a power router as shown in Fig 4. A longer wooden guide has been screwed to the guide fence to help maintain a straight run when starting and finishing each cut. Alternatively, the grooves could be hand sawn then chiselled out – whichever is preferred. In either case a secure push fit is required.

Fig 4 Routing the grooves for the legs: note the longer wooden guide screwed to the router fence

Fig 5 Checking the joints for fit

Assembly

Dry assemble all the finished components upside down on a flat, smooth surface. Bradawl through the screw holes in the brackets, then insert the screws and tighten up lightly. All the sharp edges can now be slightly rounded off with 240 grit paper before preparing for final assembly. Glue and cramp as shown in Fig 6, tighten up the screws, and leave overnight to set. After removing the cramps, sand off any blemishes and excess glue ready for finishing.

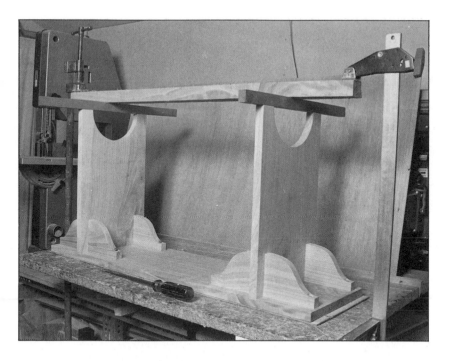

Fig 6 The bench glued and cramped ready for screws

Finishing

In the earlier days the Shakers simply covered their furniture with protective coats of paint, but soon developed oil and water stains which, when varnished and polished, preserved the natural appearance of the wood. Consequently, examples of both types of finish can still be seen, and preference is a matter of personal choice. As cherry is such an attractive wood, I haven't had the heart to use paint. Instead, boiled linseed oil, rubbed well in and left for a few days before wax polishing, has revealed its true beauty, which will darken to a rich honey hue with age. ■

CUTTING LIST
Finished sizes in mm
Cherry

		Length	Width	Thickness
1	Seat	902	241	19
2	Legs	406	241	19
4	Brackets	273	92	19

8   1¼in Number 8 countersunk-head steel screws

Peg Rails and Knobs

One of the most easily recognisable features of a
Shaker home was the peg rail. Spanning the walls of
virtually every room and corridor, these narrow
rails with their beautifully shaped hand-turned pegs
provided the means of storage essential to the
Shakers' passion for order.

THE RAILS WERE SIMPLY nailed to the lath and plaster walls, usually
at a height around two metres from the floor. Double rows
were required in areas frequented by greater numbers, such as
entrance halls and corridors, with up to three rows in the larger halls
of the communities' central meeting houses. These would be used
mainly for clothing such as hats, bonnets, coats and cloaks with a
candlesconce (see page 56) or clock appropriately placed in a
suitable position.

In other rooms mops, brooms, baskets, mirrors (see page 48),
cupboards, racks for plates and pipes, in fact almost every
conceivable domestic and industrial utensil, would have been seen
hanging in its appointed place on the peg rail.

A shorter, narrower version was often installed below the window
frames. Known as sill boards, these were usually fitted with three
equally spaced smaller pegs at a height more suitable for seated
workers.

The plainly moulded rails were mainly of knot-free pine, though
other woods including walnut are known to have been used
occasionally. They were drilled at regular intervals to accommodate
the maple or cherry pegs which projected 50mm to 75mm, about
the same average width as the rails. Often these holes would be
threaded, the matching peg shafts sometimes being screwed right
through into the wall at the back, presumably for more strength.

Both stained and painted finishes were used, varying considerably
in colour and quality. The stains ranged from a dull, semi-opaque
brown in some locations to a transparent bright orange in others.
Yellow ochre paint was obviously well liked in many dwellings, while
a blue which varied between dark green and Prussian blue was used
universally in meeting houses.

Knobs and pulls were made in a great variety of shapes and sizes with the same woods and similar mushroom-shaped heads as the rail pegs. Not only were they required for the doors and drawers of separate pieces, including desks, tables, benches, clocks and chests, but also for those incorporated into the vast expanses of fitted furniture.

An indication of the enormous numbers produced is given in the records of storage units built into the following Church Family Dwellings: Enfield, New Hampshire – 860 built-in drawers; Hancock, Massachusetts – 245 cupboard doors, 369 drawers; Canterbury, New Hampshire – 6 closets, 14 cupboards and 101 drawers were built into the attic area alone.

These figures clearly illustrate the Shakers' ability to produce in large quantities, but what is more impressive is the quality of the craftsmanship and design they were prepared to apply even to the tiniest little knob. Whether it was one-off, 500, or 1000, every delicately hand-turned peg, knob or pull had a rare charm which was characteristically Shaker.

Fig 1 The pleasing shape and balanced proportions of these museum-measured door knobs and drawer pulls, shown here full size, are evidence of the Shakers' concern with both the aesthetic and functional qualities of their work

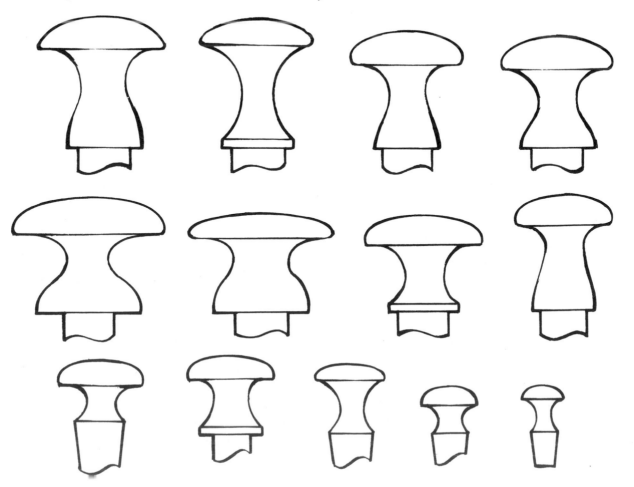

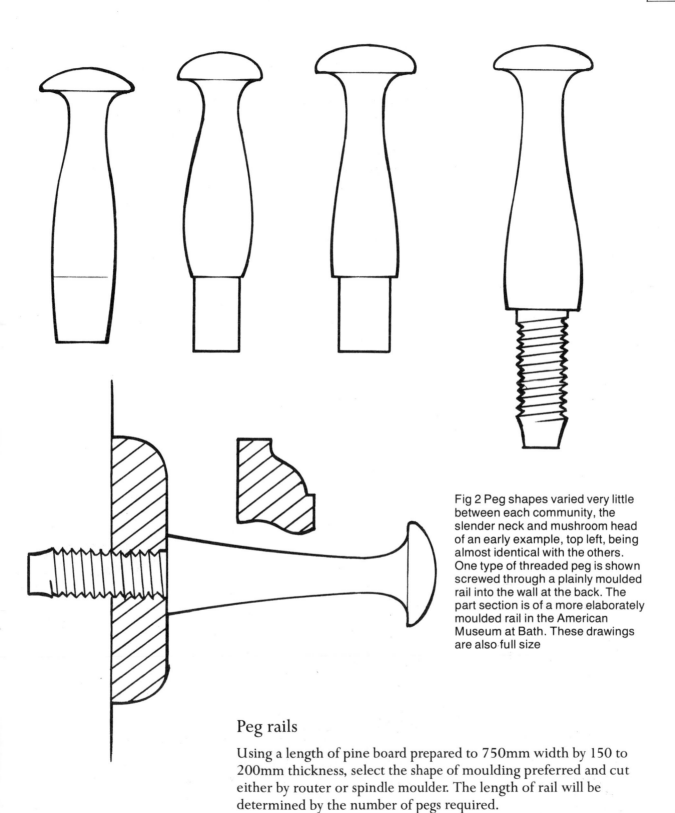

Fig 2 Peg shapes varied very little between each community, the slender neck and mushroom head of an early example, top left, being almost identical with the others. One type of threaded peg is shown screwed through a plainly moulded rail into the wall at the back. The part section is of a more elaborately moulded rail in the American Museum at Bath. These drawings are also full size

Peg rails

Using a length of pine board prepared to 750mm width by 150 to 200mm thickness, select the shape of moulding preferred and cut either by router or spindle moulder. The length of rail will be determined by the number of pegs required.

A plainly moulded example is shown in the photograph at the beginning of the chapter. The whole thing is 1070mm long and consists of five pegs positioned 50mm from each end with a 240mm space between centres. 12mm diameter holes are drilled through the rail to accommodate pegs with parallel shafts.

Wrought iron nails were originally used by the Shakers to secure the rails to their lath and plaster walls; rawlplugs and steel countersunk-head screws would be more appropriate in present day dwellings. Screw head recesses can be filled, sanded flush and polished after screwing the completed assembly to the wall.

Pegs, knobs and pulls

Blanks are rough turned between centres from cherry or maple offcuts, allowing approximately 2mm on the head diameter and 35mm on the length.

To ensure accurate repetition when producing pegs, knobs or pulls, cut out two card templates (Figs 3 and 4) using the scale drawings as a guide. Turn the shaft first, using a pre-drilled piece of scrapwood to check for fit.

The head is turned next, measured by calipers set to the finished diameter. The body can now be shaped and sanded smooth, checking regularly with Template 1 as shown in Fig 3.

Part off the shaft to a length equalling the thickness of the rail then saw off the waste at the head. Holding the peg shaft in a chuck, round off and sand the head, remembering to use Template 2 as a guide.

Fig 3 Shape the peg body between centres, using Template 1 to ensure accurate repetition

Fig 4 Checking with Template 2 when rounding off the head

Finishing

I have applied oil to the rail and pegs, leaving a natural finish before wax polishing.

   Pegs can be finished more easily on the lathe before finally gluing or threading to the rail. ∎

Looking Glasses

Shaker-made looking glasses were first produced in
the 1820s using a wide variety of woods including
maple, pine, mahogany, cherry and walnut. Rules
stated that the frames must be plain, and in an
attempt to discourage vanity, were not to exceed
18 inches in height by 12 inches width. They were
hung from pegs as described in
Pegs Rails and Knobs.

THE THREE EXAMPLES SHOWN, reproduced in cherry with pine or ply frame backs, include a hand looking glass and two types of pegged hangers. The tiny pegs were used to support combs and brushes. Resting on the hanger shelf, the angle of each mirror can be tilted and set to the required position by adjusting the supporting cord. This is another typically functional Shaker design which will require mitring, moulding and turning skills to produce.

Preparation

In the cutting list the frame sizes are shown in brackets above the section measurements. The initial prepared sizes required will be determined by the method chosen to rebate and shape the mouldings.

To ease routing the rebates freehand, and cutting the rounded moulding of the large mirror frame (see Fig 1), I have prepared material for each frame to double widths plus an allowance of 3mm waste for bandsawing into two and planing to finished widths (Fig 2).

Off-cuts from the frames and hanger shelves can be used to make the pegs.

I advise having the plain glass mirrors cut after the frames have been assembled just in case any errors occur when cutting the mitres.

Fig 1 Routing the frames

Fig 2 Halving the double width frame mouldings

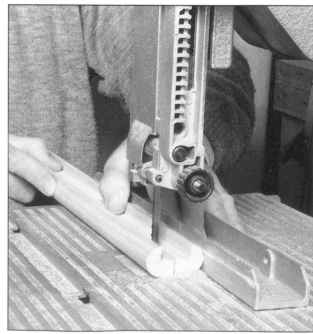

Frames

Using the dimensions shown in Figs 3 (a) and (b), cut the rebates for the mirrors. A second rebate will need to be cut for the hand looking glass frame to accommodate the back/handle.

Using a rounding over cutter, shape the large frame moulding. The chamfers of the looking glass frame can be cut with a smoothing plane.

There are many ways to cut mitres and equally as many gadgets available to help frame clamping; the choice of method must be the one for which you are best equipped. After marking out, I have rough cut the mitres on the bandsaw, then sanded up to the line on the disc sander with the guide fence set at 45°.

When satisfied with the accuracy of the joints, glue and clamp the frames, ideally using a system which incorporates right-angled corner jaws. When the glue has set, clean up the frames. Then, allowing 1mm clearance around the glass, have the mirrors cut to size.

Fig 3(a) Sectional view of small hanger

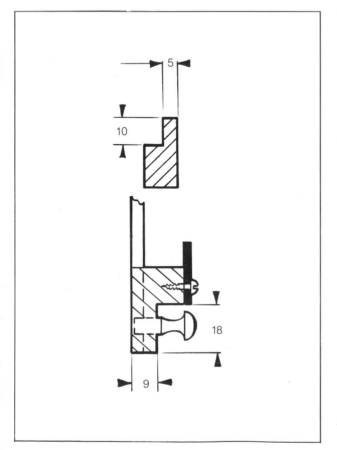

Fig 3(b) Sectional view of large hanger

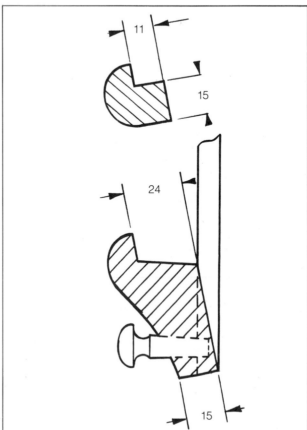

The frame backs can now be cut to fit the rebates. Using Fig 4 as a guide, make a card template to mark out the back for the hand looking glass. Lay the finished back in position and mark out the shoulder recess of the frame. Cut the angled shoulders with a fine-toothed saw then clean out with a chisel to give a nice flush fit.

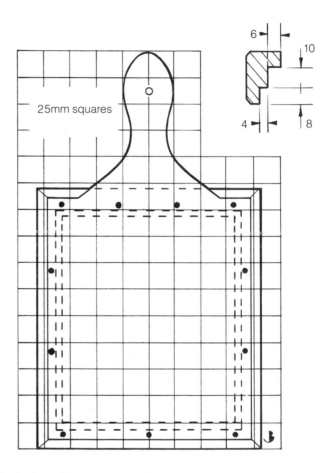

25mm squares

Fig 4 Back view of hand looking glass

Hangers

Starting with the smaller pegged hanger, mark out and shape the back. The sides start to taper 125mm from the base, blending in with the 40mm diameter rounded top.

Drill the 2mm diameter cord holes 25mm apart, 65mm from the top, and the 10mm diameter peg hole 35mm from the top. Mark out and cut the full lap T joint of the shelf, checking with the hanger back for fit.

Using a circular saw or router, cut the rebated section of the shelf as shown in Fig 3(a). Both back and shelf can now be glued and cramped.

When set, clean up all surfaces and slightly round off any sharp edges before marking out the position of the three peg holes, one in the centre and one 30mm from each end of the shelf. Drill the holes 6mm diameter, taking care not to break through at the back.

Using tin-snips or a hacksaw, cut out the two small latches which hold the mirror frame base in position. These are rounded off at the top using a file or grindstone then drilled with a 3mm diameter bit for the screws.

The larger hanger back has parallel sides, the 6mm diameter cord hole being drilled in the centre of the 26mm radius rounded top. Two further cord holes, 2mm diameter, are drilled 35mm apart 85mm from the top.

The lap T joint of the shelf is cut at an angle as shown in Fig 3(b), then cleaned up with a chisel (see Fig 5).

A good tight fit is necessary so that when dry assembled and laid flat, the shelf can be held securely at the correct angle while vertically drilling the three peg holes. These 8mm diameter holes are marked out 30mm from each end and one in the centre, with a starting point 17mm from the base. Care must be taken to prevent the drill bit wandering out of line.

Remove the hanger back and cut the angled rebate of the shelf. This can be done quite easily on the circular saw. To shape the curved front profile I have used a smoothing plane, then finished off with sandpaper before gluing and cramping back to the shelf.

Fig 5 Finishing off the large hanger shelf angled lap joint

Fig 6 Rounding off the peg head

Pegs

The tiny pegs of the smaller hanger must be among the smallest made by the Shaker craftsmen: 23mm long with head, neck and shaft diameters of 11mm, 4mm and 6mm respectively.

The heads were invariably mushroom-shaped, with shafts sometimes being tapered for a friction fit as shown in the section detail of the larger hanger in Fig 3(b). I have turned parallel shafts but this feature is optional.

The larger pegs are 35mm long with head, neck and shaft diameters 17mm, 6mm and 9mm respectively. The shaft and neck are turned first, then reversed in the chuck to shape and sand the head (Fig 6). When complete, all the pegs can be glued and left to set.

Finishing and assembly

Apply boiled linseed oil to all pieces, rub well into the wood and leave for several days before wax polishing. The mirrors can now be assembled and the backs pinned to the frames (Figs 7 and 8).

Fig 7 Pinning the back to the large frame: note recesses cut for pins

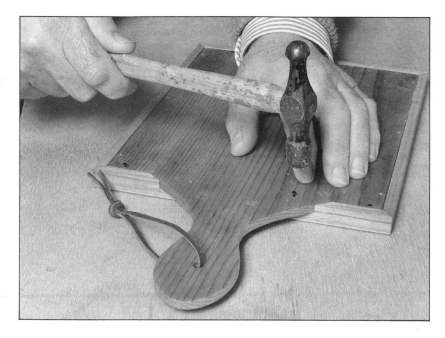

Fig 8 Pinning the hand looking
glass back

Using round-headed ½in Number 4 screws, secure the two latches
to the front side of the small hanger shelf, positioned 50mm from
each end. I have used leather thong for the hand mirror but cord as
used on the pegged hangers is equally suitable. This cord has been
threaded through 15mm screw eyes fixed to the tops of each mirror
frame, then arranged as shown in the illustrations and adjusted
to suit.

Pegged wall rails which were used to support the original looking
glasses are found on page 42. ■

CUTTING LIST
Finished sizes in mm
Cherry and Pine

	Large	Small	Hand
Frame	(419×305) 23×23	(204×152) 25×12	(248×216) 25×16
Back	389×275×6 (ply)	174×122×4 (ply)	378×202×6 (pine)
Hanger back	543×51×8	403×64×5	
Hanger shelf	305×60×34	248×32×20	
Mirror	387×273 ×3	172×120×3	212×180×3
2 sheet metal latches		25×12×1.5	

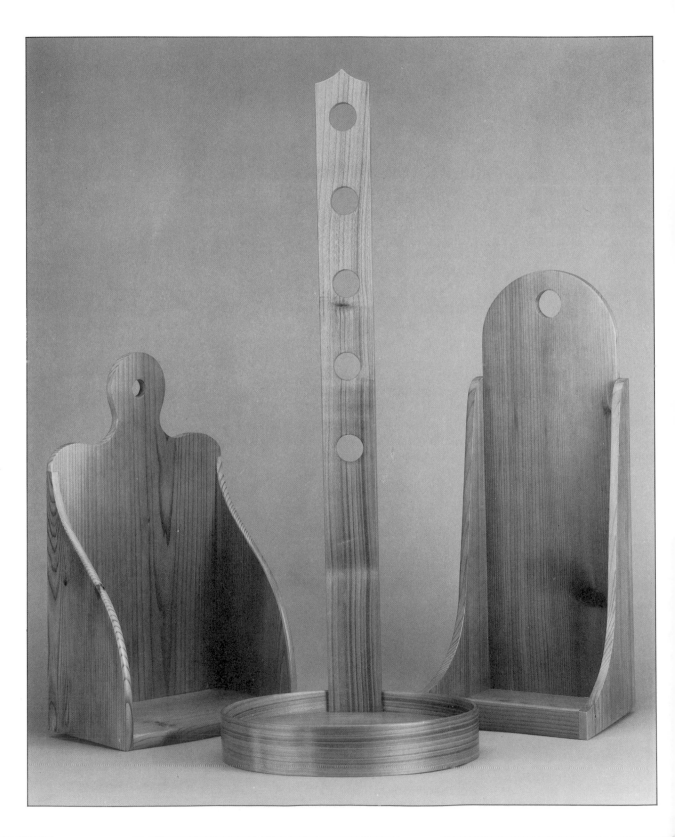

Hanging Candlesconces

Large quantities of hanging candlesconces were needed by the Shakers. They were produced in many shapes and sizes and designed to hang from the pegged wall rails. Each would support one, and in some cases two, metal candleholders known as 'hog scrapers'. Walnut, butternut, pine and cherry were among the woods used, with an even greater variety of finishes including paints, stains, varnishes and oils.

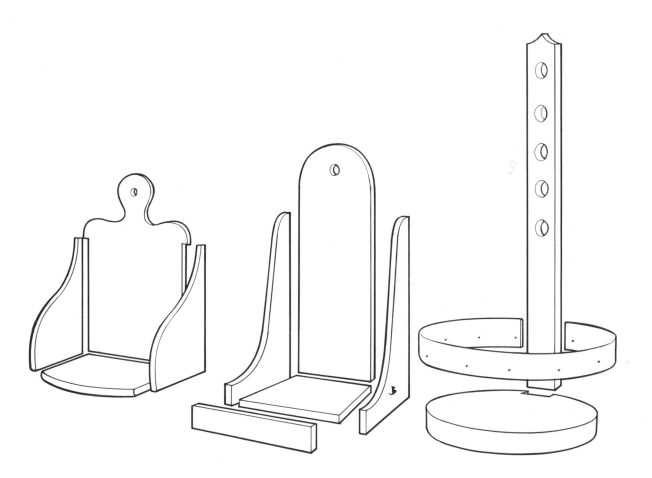

TWO OF THE THREE sconces shown here have been reproduced in pine from examples made at the Harvard and New Lebanon community workshops. The third, a longer, adjustable sconce from Pleasant Hill, Kentucky, has been reproduced in cherry.

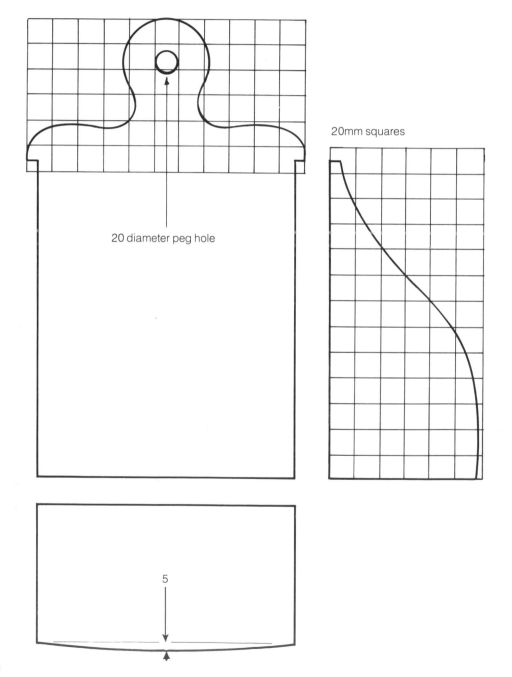

20mm squares

20 diameter peg hole

5

Fig 1 Harvard sconce

Harvard and New Lebanon sconces

With the exception of the 12mm thick base for the Harvard sconce, all pieces are cut from boards prepared to 8mm thickness. Guided by Figs 1 and 2, mark out and cut the pieces to size and shape, taking particular care when planing the correct angles for the New Lebanon sconce (Fig 3). A drum sander is ideal for shaping the concave profiles and a disc sander for the convex.

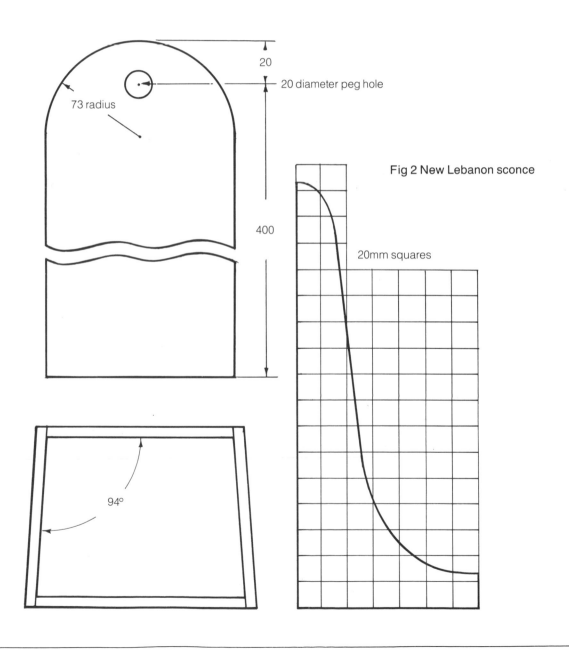

20

20 diameter peg hole

73 radius

Fig 2 New Lebanon sconce

400

20mm squares

94°

Drill out the peg holes with a flat bit. The front edges of the base and sides of the Harvard sconce are sanded round by hand, blending the top edge of the sides flush with the recessed back as shown in Fig 4. The edges on the New Lebanon sconce are square and only slightly dulled when finish sanding.

A very similar example from the same community can be seen in the Shaker collection at the American Museum, Bath. This has been made in butternut with all the upper edges rounded off. Such small variations in design were obviously tolerated by the Elders, so the choice is available.

Lay all pieces in position and check for fit before gluing and cramping. When set, clean up all surfaces with fine sandpaper, dulling any sharp edges ready for finishing.

Fig 3 The angled faces need to be accurately planed

Fig 4 Blend in the top edges with the recessed back

Pleasant Hill sconce

Five equally spaced peg holes in the back rail (see Fig 5) enabled the height of this sconce to be adjusted for convenience. Mark the centres and drill out with a 30mm flat bit (Fig 6). Mark out the 40mm radius curves of the pointed top, bandsaw, then sand smooth as with the insides of the drilled holes. Bandsaw the circular base, leaving just enough material to disc sand accurately to the line. Mark out the recess which will accommodate the back rail, making sure that the direction of grain is as shown in the 'Plan of base', Fig 5. Cut out with a saw and chisel to provide a firm fit. Shape the projecting corners of the rail bottom flush with the circumference of the base – this will allow the rim to blend in neatly at the back when finally assembling. Glue and cramp the rail in the base recess.

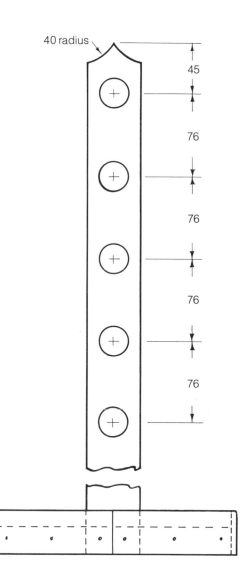

40 radius

45

76

76

76

76

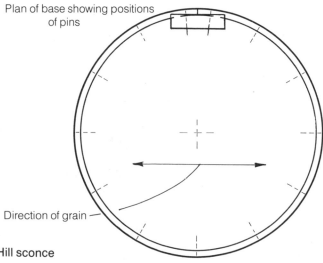

Plan of base showing positions of pins

Direction of grain

Fig 5 Pleasant Hill sconce

Fig 6 Drill from both sides with the flat bit

Fig 7 Cramp the soaked band round the disc and leave to dry

Cut the side strip to length, then round off the top rim with a smoothing plane and sandpaper. An extra 10mm has been included in the length to allow for bending. Immerse the strip in hot water and leave for approximately 2 hours. While this is soaking, bandsaw a 240mm diameter disc from the centre of a piece of scrapwood 300mm square by 40 to 50mm thick. The off-cuts will serve as cramps.

Wrap the flexible soaked strip firmly round the disc then tighten up in the vice with the cramps positioned as shown in Fig 7. Leave to dry for a couple of days.

Place the now dry circular band round the base, mark off the overlap and cut to finished length. Using a 1mm diameter bit, pre-drill the pin holes 13mm up from the bottom edge. Sand the sides smooth before gluing and pinning, taking care to position the ends at the centre of the rail back. Remove any surplus glue, sand the bottom flat and smooth, then dull the outer edge ready for finishing.

Very similar sconces with a one-piece base were produced at the Union Village community, Ohio. These have a thicker rim, formed by recessing the centre of the base on the lathe. If preferred, this method could be adopted as an alternative.

Finishing

Sconces were often stained an orange red before varnishing. However, both colour and medium varied enormously depending on the location. The examples shown have been left their natural colour, sealed with clear varnish, then rubbed down lightly with fine steel wool before wax polishing. ■

CUTTING LIST
Finished sizes in mm
Cherry or Pine

		Harvard	New Lebanon	Pleasant Hill
1	Back	360×220×8	420×146×8	632×51×12
2	Sides	247×117×8	325×140×8	740×44×5
1	Base	204×117×12	163×125×8	222dia.×25
1	Front		165×25×8	
13	gimp pins 18mm long			

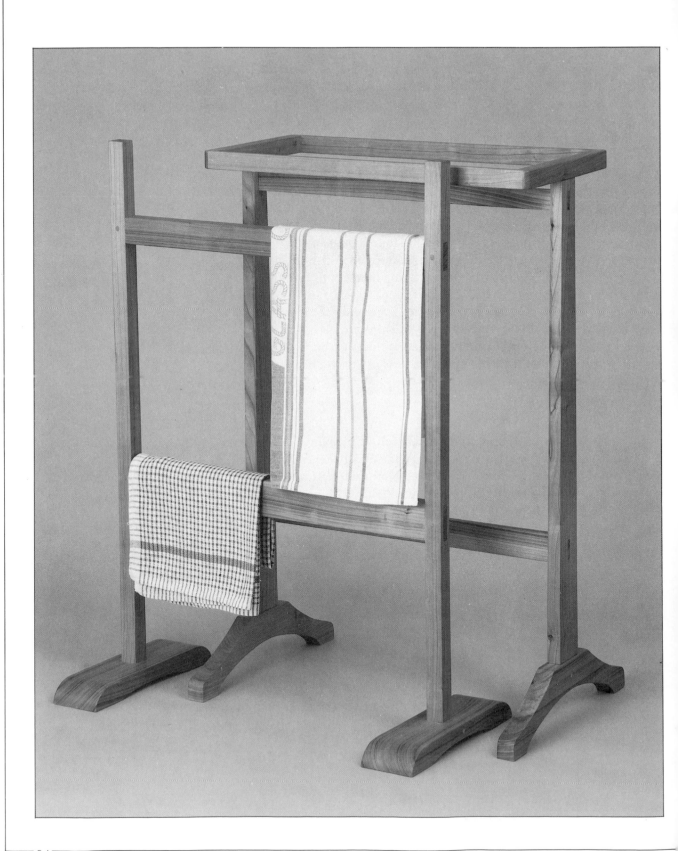

Drying Stands

Various types of drying stands were produced in the
Shaker communities. Some were freestanding,
others hung from peg rails on the walls. Although
pine was more commonly used, the examples
shown here have been made in a slightly heavier,
more contrastingly figured cherry without
noticeably affecting their remarkable lightness in weight.

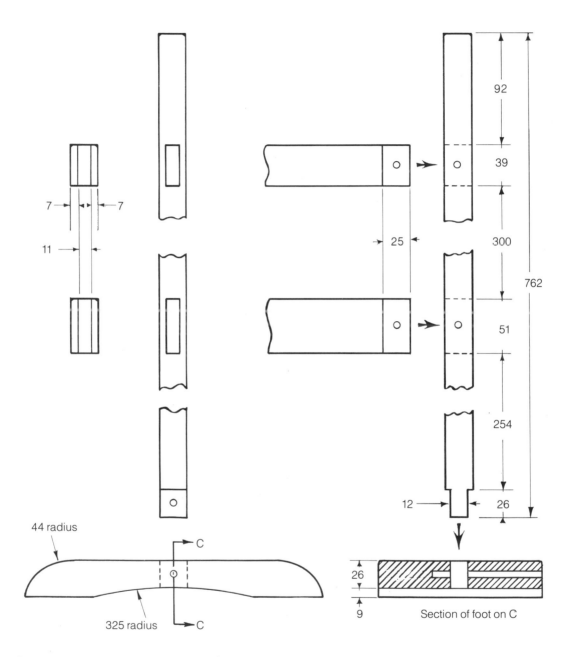

7 ← →◄ ►← 7

11 → ◄

92

39

300

762

25

51

254

12 →

26

44 radius

C

325 radius C

26

9

Section of foot on C

Fig 1 Stand 1, the Harvard Drying Stand

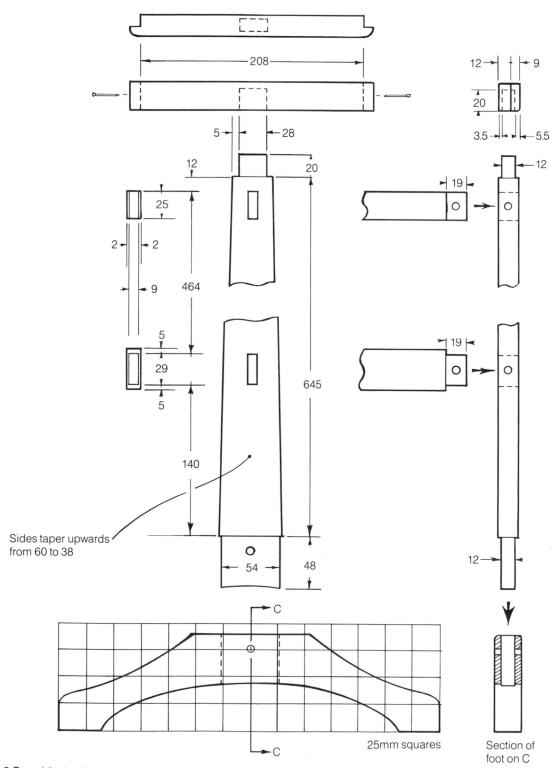

5

28

12

20

25

2

2

9

464

5

29

5

645

140

Sides taper upwards
from 60 to 38

54

48

208

12

9

20

3.5

5.5

19

12

19

12

C

C

25mm squares

Section of
foot on C

Fig 2 Stand 2, the Hancock Drying Stand

T HESE TYPICALLY PLAIN, practical pieces are deceptively simple in appearance. To provide ultimate strength, all the stile to rail joints are pegged-through tenons, which are a test of skill to the most experienced craftsman.

Feet

Mark out the profile of each foot. For the feet of Stand 2, make a card template using the scaled drawing (Fig 2) as a guide (Fig 3). Bandsaw the bottom curve only, then sand off smooth before marking out the mortises on both flat top and lower curved surfaces. Waste from the mortises can be removed either completely by mallet and firmer chisel, working from each end until the cuts meet in the middle – Method 1 (see Fig 4), or by drilling through with a dowel bit and then cleaning out with a chisel – Method 2, (see Figs 4 and 5).

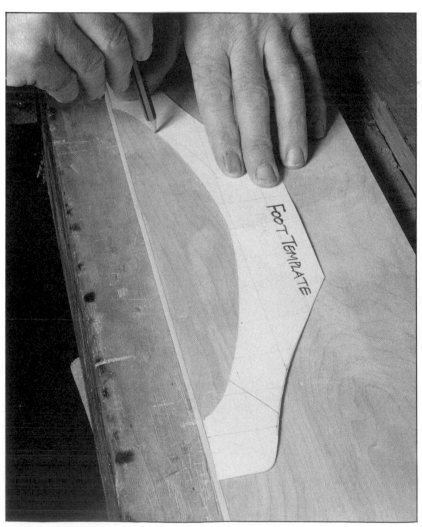

Fig 3 Using the template to mark out feet for Stand 2

I favoured the second method, using the dowel bit in a pillar drill and taking care to break through very slowly to avoid splintering the bottom face. To provide more stability and maintain a vertical position during this operation, the narrower feet of Stand 2 were clamped together. When the mortises have been completed, finish off shaping the feet by bandsaw, then chamfer the top edges and sand smooth.

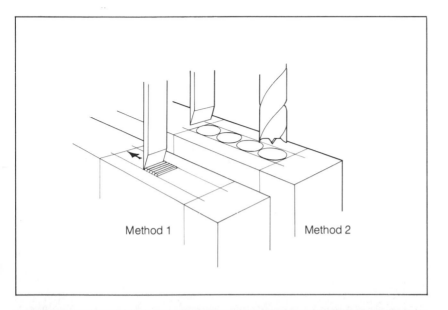

Method 1   Method 2

Fig 4 Removing waste from mortises

Fig 5 Cleaning up the mortises after drilling out

Stiles

On both sides of each stile, mark out and cut the mortises as for the feet but cramp firmly to a solid bench top when chiselling. The tenons are marked out next then very carefully cut to provide a smooth but firm fit. This type of joint is demanding and any indiscretion committed in the making is unfortunately visible for all to see. The following Shaker saying is worth considering, 'Do your work as though you had a thousand years to live, and as if you were to die tomorrow.'

Of the many ways to cut tenons, I have chosen to remove the waste by saw, then clean up with a chisel for final fit. Dry assemble the feet, rails and stiles of both stands, mark out the peg centres and check all joints for fit.

Before progressing to the top frame of Stand 2, rough saw the tapered sides of the stiles and finish up to the line with a smoothing plane. Mark out and cut the 20mm deep mortises of the top frame ends, checking for fit before cutting the rebates which accommodate the frame sides. Round off the 9mm radius corners then glue, cramp and pin (Fig 6).

Fig 6 The top frame of Stand 2 in cramps

Fig 7 Smoothing off foot joints after gluing and pegging

Assembly

Before assembly, cut all the dowels to length, adding 2mm extra for each projecting end. Glue and sash-cramp stiles to feet. Lay a flat piece of scrapwood under each foot, hold down firmly and drill the dowel holes. Sand a slight chamfer on the lead edge of each dowel, glue and fit leaving 1mm projecting from each side of the joint. When set, plane off flush and sand smooth (Fig 7). Glue and cramp the rails next (Fig 8), checking at each stage for squareness, then repeat the dowelling operation. After allowing sufficient time for the glue to set, remove the cramps before planing flush the through joints and projecting dowels. The top frame can now be glued and cramped to Stand 2. Finally, finish sand all surfaces and any remaining sharp edges, slightly rounding off the rails' top edges.

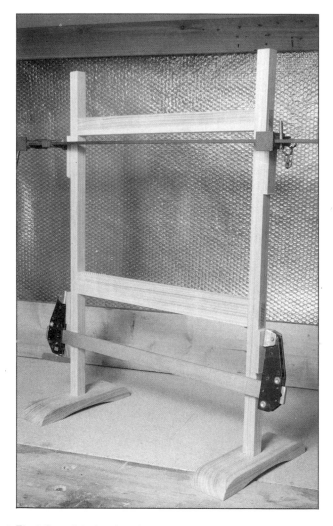

Fig 8 Stand 1 glued and cramped: note that the position of packing pieces avoids the ends of the tenons

Fig 9 Underside of the foot showing through tenon detail after sanding

Finishing

Whether made in cherry or pine, polyurethane gloss varnish is the most practical finish for these drying stands. When the varnish is hardened I prefer to rub down the gloss lightly with fine wire wool, then apply wax polish which gives a more mellow, natural appearance and feel. ∎

Fig 10 Completed stands ready for finishing

CUTTING LIST
Finished sizes in mm
Cherry or Pine

		Harvard	Hancock
2	Feet	280×76×35	350×92×25
2	Stiles	762×25×25	713×64×19
2	Top rails	521×39×25	495×25×13
2	Bottom rails	521×51×25	495×39×13
2	Top frame sides		476×25×10
2	Top frame ends		228×25×21

1 metre length of 6mm diameter dowelling
4 steel pins 12.5mm long

Canterbury Step Chest

This small step chest has been reproduced from an example in the Shaker Museum, Old Chatham, New York. Step chests were actually used as footstools. Seated with legs crossed and one foot on each level, the knees were raised to a convenient height when either reading or sewing. The lidded compartment was used to accommodate sewing materials.

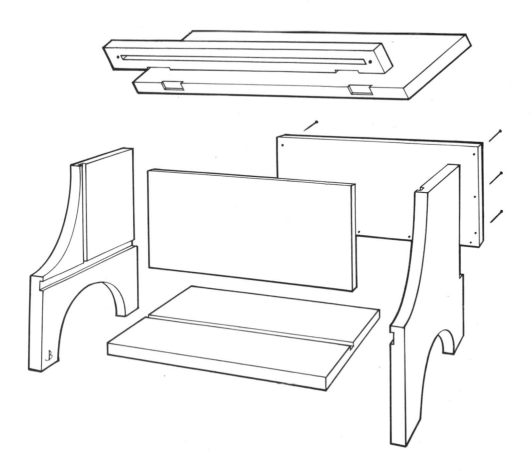

T HE SHAKERS COMMONLY used a variety of different woods in their furniture. As illustrated in this example, soft pine for the front and back panels has been combined with the harder cherry used for the remaining parts which would have been subjected to most wear.

Preparation

Apart from the front and back, all the pieces are made from cherry board prepared to 16mm thickness. For the front and back I have used a pine panel salvaged from an old drawer bottom then planed down to 8mm thickness. 5/16

Mark out all the pieces and cut to the sizes shown in the cutting list. It is important to ensure that all surfaces are flat, edges square and sanded smooth.

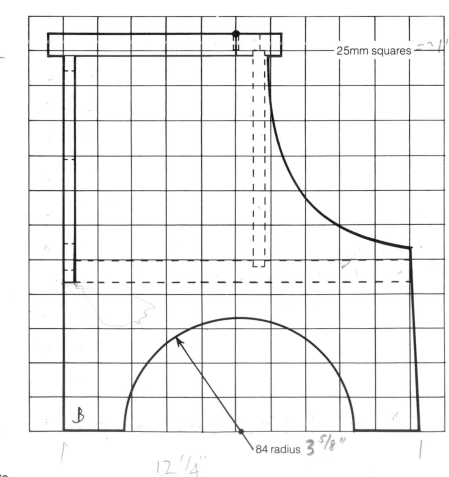

25mm squares

84 radius 3 5/8"

Fig 1 Side piece template

Sides

On a piece of thin card make a full-size template of the side, using Fig 1 as a guide. Mark the outlines and the positions of the grooves on the insides of both side pieces.

Two thin plywood packing pieces are clamped to the work surface to act as stops to prevent the work piece from sliding around when routing. Cut the 16mm wide horizontal grooves in each side piece, locating the router guide on the bottom edge. The 8mm wide vertical grooves are cut next, using the back edge for guide location.

The outlines can now be cut by bandsaw or fretsaw. Clean up the back edges with a chisel, smooth off the sloping fronts with a plane, and the curves can be finished with a drum sander.

Step, top and lid

Mark out the position of the 8mm wide groove in the step and, before cutting (Fig 2), check for line-up with the corresponding vertical grooves of the side pieces.

The top and lid are one piece at this stage, which makes routing of the 8mm wide top groove more controllable. Cut the groove to within 24mm of each end then clean out square with a chisel. The widths of the top and lid, 35mm and 136mm respectively, can now be marked out, sawn and planed to size. Sufficient material has been allowed in the cutting list for this operation.

Fig 2 Routing the step groove

Fig 3 Sides, step and top grooves completed

Fig 4 Checking the butt hinge recesses for fit

Mark out the positions of the butt hinges 70mm from the ends, then saw and chisel out the recesses. Check for fit (Fig 4) and, if this is satisfactory, bradawl the screw holes.

Assembly

Dry assemble all the pieces as shown in Fig 5. Ideally, the step ends should be a comfortable fit in the side pieces and the front panel an easy push fit in its respective grooves. The top edge of the step front should project slightly, and this can be skimmed off after final assembly. Mark off and pre-drill the pin positions, one at each end of the top piece for 1½in long pins, and seven in the back panel for 1in pins.

Fig 5 Dry assembly

The nails originally used were hand-wrought, progressing later to machine-made. When hammered in, the heads were left visible, flush with the wood. Using the bright steel panel pins of today, it would be preferable to punch the heads in slightly and either use a filler or progressive coats of polish to conceal the heads.

The assembly can now be glued, cramped and pinned as shown in Fig 6, checking for squareness at each stage. Leave it to set overnight before assembling the hinged top, then clean up all the surfaces ready for finishing.

Fig 6 Final assembly, checking for squareness at each stage

Finishing

Preferring a natural finish, I have used boiled linseed oil, rubbed well into the grain and left for several days before finally wax polishing. ∎

CUTTING LIST
Finished sizes in mm
Pine and Cherry

		Length	Width	Thickness	
2	Sides	272	260	16 ⎫	
1	Step	341	246	16 ⎬ **Cherry**	
1	Top lid	390	175	16 ⎭	
1	Front	341	157	8 ⎫ **Pine**	
1	Back	365	165	8 ⎭	

1 pair of butt hinges 1½ in × ½ in

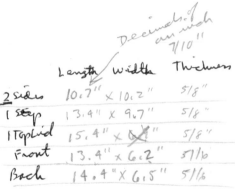

Decimals of an inch 7/10"

	Length	Width	Thickness
2 Sides	10.7"	10.2"	5/8"
1 Step	13.4"	9.7"	5/8"
1 Toplid	15.4"	⨯8"	5/8"
Front	13.4"	6.2"	5/16
Back	14.4"	6.5"	5/16

Adjustable Candlesconce

Candlelight was very important to the Shakers,
especially as their working day started at 4.30 in the
morning. The many types of holders they produced
were largely designed to hang from pegged wall
rails. This free-standing candlesconce, made in
cherry, was primarily for use in their workshops.

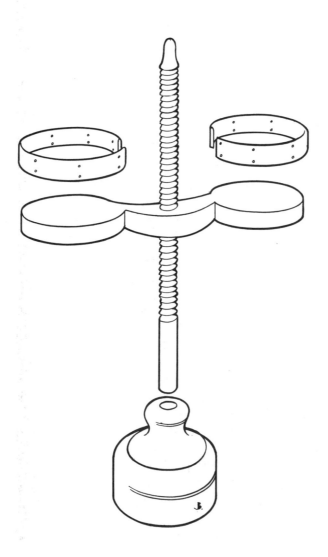

T WO CANDLES, each held in a Shaker-made metal candlestick, would rest on either end of the swivel arm. By revolving the swivel, the height could be adjusted to suit any working position.

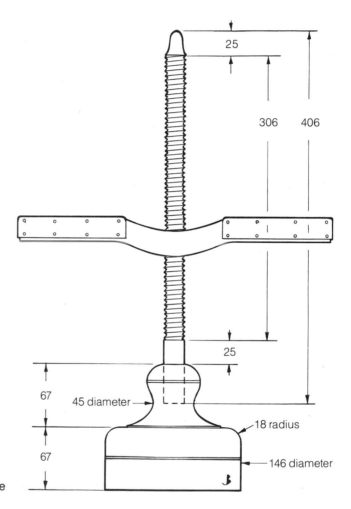

Fig 1 Dimensioned views of the candlesconce

Base

The base has been made from one piece of cherry, with the grain running vertically. If this size is not available, pieces will have to be glued together to provide the required width.

Mark out a 150mm diameter circle on the face of each end and roughly shape ready for turning. Drill a hole 20mm deep in the centre of one end to accommodate a screw chuck, then assemble on the lathe. The projecting end, which is to be the bottom of the base, is squared off, sanded smooth and drilled for repositioning on the screw chuck. Using the drawing as a guide, turn the base to finished size (Fig 2) then sand smooth before cutting the 1mm deep groove lines. The post hole can now be drilled, either on the lathe, as shown in Fig 3, or on the bench.

Fig 2 Shaping the base

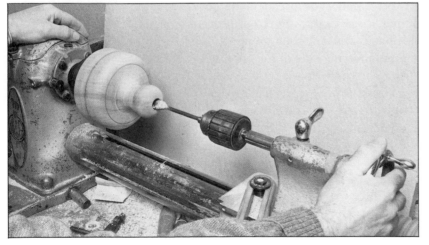

Fig 3 Drilling the post hole

Post

Centre each end of the post and turn between centres, leaving 1mm on the diameter. This must be removed very carefully to achieve smooth parallel sides. It could normally be done by using sandpaper wrapped round a flat block, but as the residual grit would cause wear on the threadcutter I have deviated by using a smoothing plane.

Set the plane for a small cut and hold firmly at around 45° to the post's centre axis. By lightly stroking the top side of the revolving spindle, a smooth flat surface will be obtained.

Fig 4 Cutting the pole threads by rotating the end faceplate

During this operation it is easier to control the plane by locating its sole on a long toolrest set at a level just above centre.

Turn a lead taper at the tailstock end to ease cutting the first threads. Then, bearing in mind that sufficient material has been allowed for waste at each end of the spindle, mark out the length to be threaded.

Most suppliers of threadcutting tools do not stock the ⅞in (22mm) diameter size cutter used to produce the original Shaker example. If this size is available then the finished diameter of the post and accommodating hole in the base will be 22mm (⅞in).

I have used the more easily available ¾in (19mm) size which does not noticeably affect the proportions or function of the finished sconce. The hole in the base was subsequently drilled to accommodate a ¾in (19mm) post.

Threadcutting is very satisfying and not the awesome task most would suspect. By following the maker's instructions, even a beginner can produce a good quality thread quickly and easily.

The thread-box can be used with the post either on the lathe or vertical at the bench. When this is done, turn and sand the top shape as much as is possible on the lathe, then mark out and cut off to finished length at the base. The rounded top end can be finish sanded by hand.

Swivel

Plane the top surface smooth and square to the sides. Then, using a piece of thin card, make a template of the top shape from Fig 6 and mark out. Drill the centre hole and an additional one in the waste area for a practice run. Holding the swivel block securely in the vice, cut the threads, remembering to check the die for squareness. Bandsaw the top shape first then sand to finished size. The side shape can now be marked out, cut and sanded.

Fig 5 Checking for squareness is important when starting to thread

Swivel

Fig 6 Dimensioned view of swivel

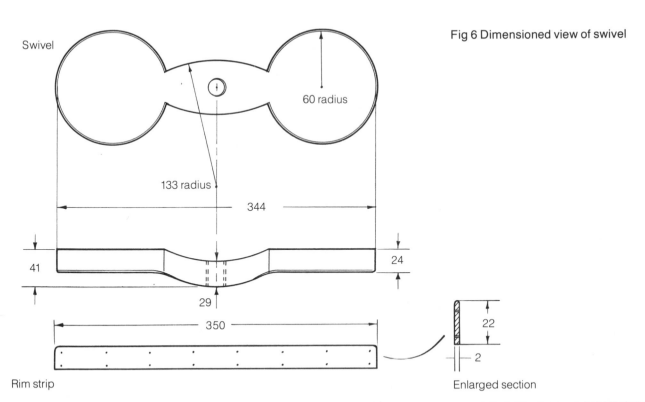

60 radius

133 radius

344

41

24

29

350

22

2

Rim strip

Enlarged section

Fig 7 Bandsaw the top shape first

Fig 8 Rim strips, before and after bending

Plane the rim strips down to finished thickness and width, then round off the top edges. Leave 2mm waste on each end of both strips before cutting to length. This allows for final adjustment prior to pinning. With a sharp point mark out the pin hole positions clearly before preparing for bending. Immerse the strips in a pan of hot water and leave to simmer on a stove. Using a piece of 50mm thick scrapwood, turn a 115mm diameter disc and leave on the lathe. After approximately 1 hour of soaking, the strips will be flexible enough to be wrapped and tied round the disc (Fig 9).

Leave overnight to dry before removing the string. Then, holding each strip on the disc, pre-drill the 1mm diameter pin holes. Secure the swivel in a vice and check the curved strips for fit, making any necessary adjustments to length prior to sanding smooth and pinning.

Fig 9 Tying the soaked rim round the disc

Assembly and finishing

The post should fit tightly in the base, with no glue required. Apply a liberal coat of boiled linseed oil, rub well into the grain and leave for several days before wax polishing. The base and post can together be buffed up to a beautiful finish on the lathe. ■

Fig 10 The parts polished ready for assembly

CUTTING LIST
Finished sizes in mm
Cherry

		Length	Width	Thickness
1	Base	152	152	152
1	Post	460	25	25
1	Swivel	355	125	43
2	Rims	354	25	4

16 gimp pins ½in japanned

Drop Leaf Table

The Shakers made several designs of maple and cherry drop leaf tables. They were usually stained light red or reddish dark brown and had an oiled or varnished finish. Some had drawers, others had only one leaf.

A RARE EXAMPLE in the American Museum, Bath, has delicately taper-turned legs which are slightly splayed to give more stability. I have reproduced this piece in birds' eye maple, sealing with oil before wax polishing. Using such spectacular wood was an act of self-indulgence on my part – harmony, economy and precision are the main ingredients behind Shaker appeal.

Preparation

Whether using cherry or maple, stable, well-seasoned timber must be selected, especially for the top. Boards of sufficient width ought to be easily available for the leaves, but the centre board could prove to be more difficult. If so, two narrower boards will have to be butt jointed and dowelled, allowing an additional 2mm on the thickness for finish planing to 19mm after gluing.

Measurements shown in the cutting list are finished sizes. Adding an extra 10mm on both ends of each leg will ease routing the mortises and allow for waste when cutting the angled tops and feet to finished length.

On a piece of stout paper, make a full-size drawing of one frame end assembly, including the full length of legs (Fig 1). This will prove invaluable when setting the correct angle of 2.5 degrees on the sliding bevel and also for checking the finished pieces for accuracy. Again with accuracy in mind, brad-pointed bits are recommended for drilling the dowel and pivot holes.

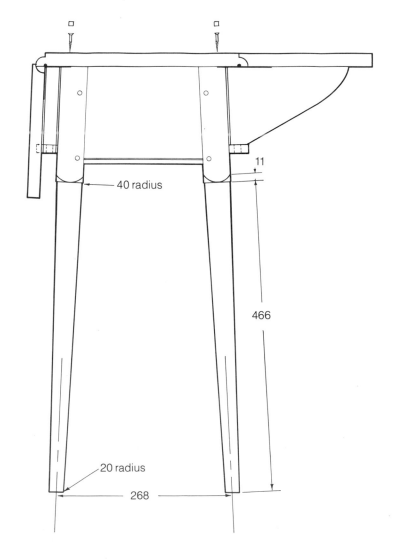

40 radius

11

466

20 radius

268

Fig 1 Frame end assembly

Fig 2 Mortise and tenon details

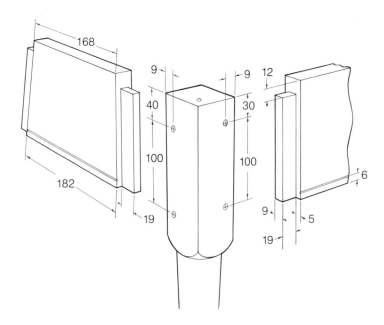

Fig 3 Routing the leg mortises

Legs

All mortise and tenon dimensions are shown in Fig 2. Check that the wood for each leg is perfectly square in section then mark out the length, allowing 10mm waste on each end. Time can be saved by marking the mortises on one leg then transferring these measurements by try-square to the others.

Hold each leg firmly in a vice and rout the blind mortises as shown in Fig 3. When the full depth of 20mm has been reached, clean out the ends with a chisel, remembering to angle the mortises which accommodate the frame end tenons.

Mark the centre on both ends of each leg ready for turning between centres. The long, straight taper is turned first followed by cutting the rounded chamfer, see Fig 4. This must be done very carefully, taking care not to splinter the corners of the squared section. Finally, sand down through the grades to a fine, smooth finish before removing from the lathe.

Fig 4 Cutting the rounded chamfer

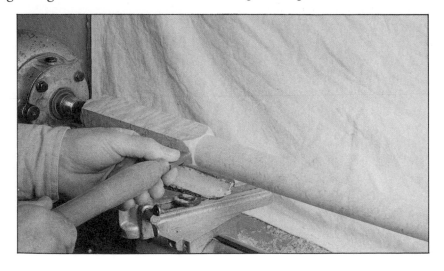

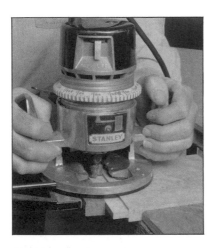

Fig 5 Routing the end tenons

Frame sides and ends

Using a router to cut the tenons (Fig 5), set the guide fence to locate on the face of each end. Particular attention must be paid to ensure that these faces are cut accurately to length and shape. Clamp each frame side and end firmly to the bench during this operation, checking with the leg mortises for fit before determining the final depth of cut.

When this is done, remove the waste from the top end of each tenon and dry assemble the two frame ends. These can now be checked against the full-size drawing before marking and bandsawing the post heads level with the top side of the frame ends. Mark out and cut the legs to length, taking care to maintain the correct angle at the feet.

Dry assemble the frame, checking all is square in plan. Before taking it apart, mark the ends of the frame sides to correspond with the tops of the post heads. Remove the sides and plane down to the lines. Mark out and cut the 12×36mm wide through-mortises which accommodate the rail ends. Set the sliding bevel to the correct angle and use it as a guide when cleaning out with the chisel.

A 1.5mm deep groove, cut into the frame sides and ends, provides a subtle decorative touch.

At this stage, glue and cramp the two end frame assemblies only (Fig 6). Allow time to set, remove the cramps and drill the dowel holes of the glued joints 6mm diameter × 22mm deep. Glue and fit the dowels, leaving the heads 1mm or so proud for cleaning up later.

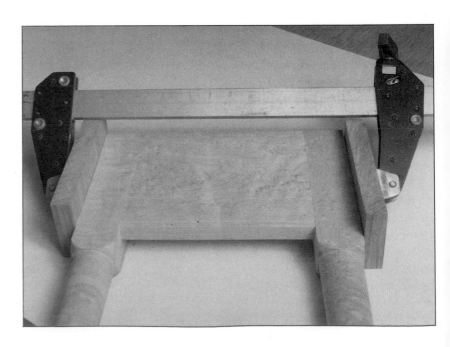

Fig 6 End frame assembly glued and cramped

Rail

Mark out the joints, checking with the full-size drawing for accuracy before cutting. Try it for fit and then as a further check dry assemble the rail and complete frame to make sure the distance between the rail's shoulder joints is correct. Mark the pivot hole centres and rounded ends, then drill the holes at the correct angle and shape the ends.

Finally, the upper side is cut to match the bottom face of the leaf support. The complete rail and frame assembly can now be glued and cramped. When the glue has set, dowel the remaining joints as with the frame ends and leave it to set. Using a smoothing plane, clean up flush all the projecting dowel heads and joints and then sand clean, slightly dulling the sharp edges of the posts, feet and undersides of the frame.

Top

Those who have not made a drop leaf table before must not be discouraged by the apparent sophistication of the rule joints. With the correct matching bits (Bosch 12.7mm cove bit and rounding over bit) these can be cut very easily by router (Figs 7 and 8).

Arrange the prepared boards to give the most pleasing effect then mark an identification line diagonally across the top faces.

To make absolutely sure the surfaces to be jointed match perfectly, I have skimmed them up using a router and straightedge guide. The guide can be cut from 6mm ply, 150mm wide by 930mm long, then hand planed dead straight the full length of one edge.

Clamp the guide and board to a bench, with the guide overhanging at each end of the board. This will enable the router base to maintain a straight path at the start and end of each cut.

Repeat this procedure when cutting the joints, but with the straightedge guide positioned just allowing the cutter guide pin to make contact with the board edge (Figs 7 and 8).

Fig 7 Cutting the rule joint out of the top

Fig 8 Cutting the leaf rule joint

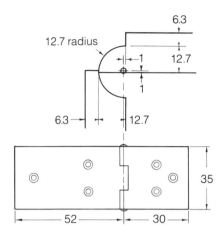

Fig 9 Hinge and rule joint details

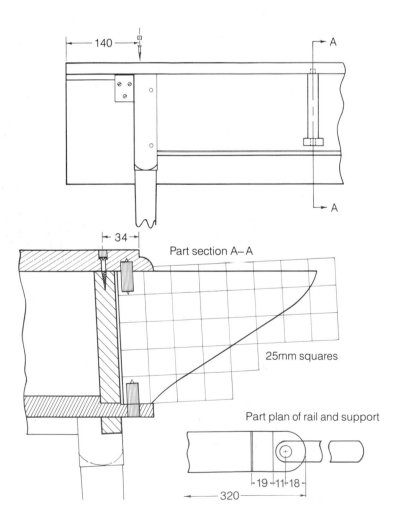

Part section A–A

25mm squares

Part plan of rail and support

Fig 10 Details of leaf supports

Lay the jointed boards upside down on a flat bench and mark out the hinge locations so that they just clear the leg posts. Fit the hinges with the pivot pin centre positioned as shown in Fig 9.

Note that when the leaf is down, its leading edge is just above that of the top. Straighten off the ends with a smoothing plane then remove the leaves before marking out the centres of the six screws which secure the top to the frame.

I suspect the Shakers used dowels only, but I shall continue with the following alternative, leaving the option open to you.

Drill the 8mm diameter plug holes 8mm deep, then straight through with a 4.5mm diameter bit to give ample clearance for a 32mm long number 8 countersunk-head steel screw. Lay the top on the frame and hold securely in the correct position using two boards, one under the frame and one on the top, both overhanging to enable cramping. Bradawl through the pre-drilled holes and drive the screws in lightly. Remove cramps and boards then place upside down and leave on the bench. From 9mm diameter dowel, cut the 9mm long plugs and put them away for later.

Leaf supports

Using Fig 10 as a guide, mark out and cut the supports, with the direction of grain running lengthwise. Plane the tops and bottoms carefully to the lines before marking the dowel hole centres. These 18mm deep holes must be drilled very accurately, ideally using a pillar drill with the support held securely in a vice.

Finish shaping then check for fit between the rail and the top as shown in Fig 11. If all is well, cut the upper and bottom pivot dowels, 26mm and 28mm long respectively. Sand a slight chamfer on the ends then glue them.

Re-fit the leaves, just lightly tightening one screw in each hinge flap. Mark out the leaf-support dowel centres and the position of the 5mm-deep recesses which accommodate the rail's projecting ends. Remove the leaves and top, chisel out the round-bottomed recesses and drill the two 10mm-deep dowel holes at the correct angle.

Assembly

Apply a thin coat of polish to the leaf support pivot dowels and their respective holes. Fit the supports into the rail ends and lower the top board into position. Screw down firmly then glue and tap home the plugs, leaving the heads slightly proud.

Before reassembling the leaves, the finish will have to be applied to the rule joints because some parts will be inaccessible afterwards. When the leaves have been fitted, allow sufficient time for the glued plugs to set then sand down the complete top flat and smooth. Slightly dull the outer edges and lower the leaves and remove all dust, especially from between the rule joints.

Finishing

As mentioned earlier, the Shakers were partial to staining their pieces before finishing with varnish or thinned, boiled linseed oil. Preferring not to use stain, I have used a proprietary brand of already thinned wood-reviving oil. This was rubbed in well and left to dry before wax polishing. ∎

Fig 11 Checking the leaf support for fit between rail and top

CUTTING LIST			
Finished sizes in mm			
Maple or Cherry	**Length**	**Width**	**Thickness**
1 Top	908	320	19
4 Legs	644	41	41
2 Frame ends	220	149	19
2 Frame sides	613	149	19
2 Leaves	908	200	19
1 Rail	320	36	19
2 Leaf supports	183	121	19

Hardwood dowel: 200×9 diameter, 400×8 diameter, 500×6 diameter
4 Drop leaf hinges 82×35

Pedestal Tables

Small pedestal tables were a familiar feature in most Shaker retiring rooms. More commonly referred to as candlestands, which describes their primary function, they could conveniently be placed where light was most needed.

T HESE TWO SPIDER legged examples, typical of those made at the New Lebanon and New Hampshire communities, represent the ultimate development in candlestand design. The fine, delicate lines contrast considerably with the primitive square-topped peg or stick-legged stands produced barely twenty years earlier.

Candlestands were usually made in cherry or maple then stained and varnished. The legs have been secured to the columns by sliding dovetails, and this traditional method of jointing pedestal tables has been further strengthened on the smaller stand by adding a metal baseplate. A spigot at the column head is simply glued to a brace which in turn is screwed to the underside of the top. Occasionally the spigot and brace was threaded, enabling the top to be easily removed.

Top

Arrange the boards to give the most interesting effect, checking that the annular rings alternate as shown in Fig 1. It is essential to form good butt joints, so shoot the edges with care then mark out for dowelling. The dowels will strengthen the joints, improve location and make gluing easier.

Position the 6mm diameter holes 50mm from each end and one in the centre. Drill the holes 15mm deep, which allows a slight clearance for each of the 28mm dowels.

Of the many adhesives available, a powdered resin wood glue is recommended – the inconvenience of having to mix it with water is compensated for by its reliability. Glue the top using two sash cramps with a weight placed on the centre to maintain flatness. Allow to set before planing and sanding down to finished thickness. The rounded edge of the rim can either be turned on the lathe, see Fig 2, or cut by router using a rounding over bit. When this is done, finish sanding the edges smooth, slightly dulling the sharp upper edge of the rim.

Fig 2 Rounding the rim on the outboard side of the headstock

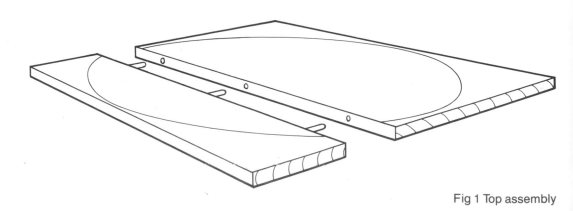

Fig 1 Top assembly

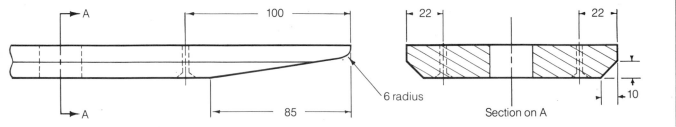

A

100

22

22

6 radius

A

85

Section on A

10

Brace

Fig 3 Brace for large stand

The brace for the small stand consists of a simple turned disc with a curved chamfer on the bottom face. This is best shaped and sanded fixed to a screw chuck on the lathe. Mark the positions of four equally spaced screw holes at a radius of 76mm from the disc centre. Drill through with a 5mm bit then countersink.

The larger stand requires a longer cross brace with planed chamfers as shown in Fig 3. Both braces will need to be drilled through the centre to accommodate the column spigot. If the spigot is to be threaded, drill the required clearance hole and cut the threads, see Fig 4. The brace can now be glued and screwed to the top, positioned centrally with the grain directions at right angles to each other.

Fig 4 Carefully maintain the cutter at right angles when threading the brace

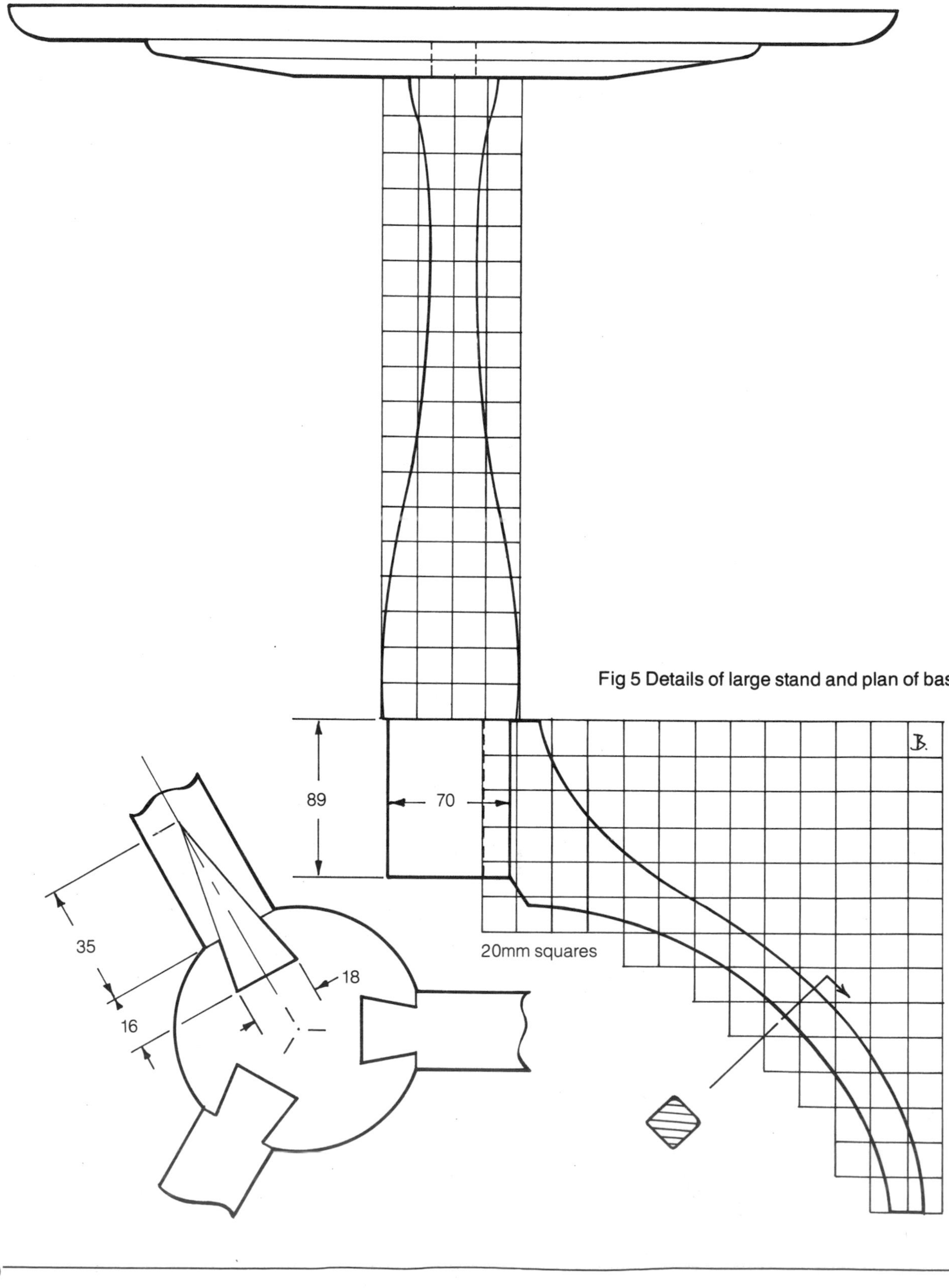

Fig 5 Details of large stand and plan of base

89

70

35

18

16

20mm squares

B.

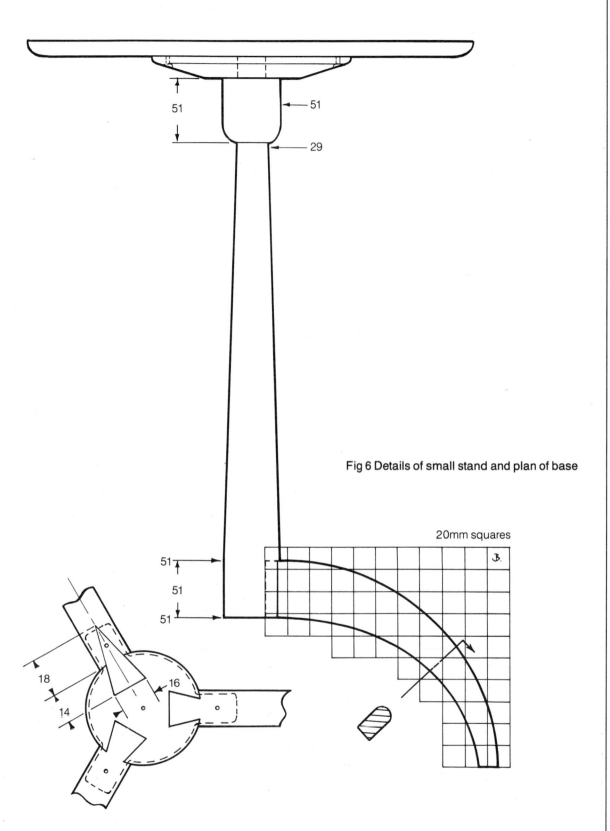

51

51

29

Fig 6 Details of small stand and plan of base

20mm squares

51

51

51

18

14

16

Column

For the following two sections, use the dimensioned drawings Figs 5 and 6, details of stands and plan of base.

To reproduce the finely balanced proportions of the column, it is necessary to check the measurements frequently for accuracy with calipers. Rough turn the column to shape, see Fig 7, leaving approximately 1mm on the diameters for final finishing. The section to be jointed is turned to finished size taking great care to maintain a flat parallel profile.

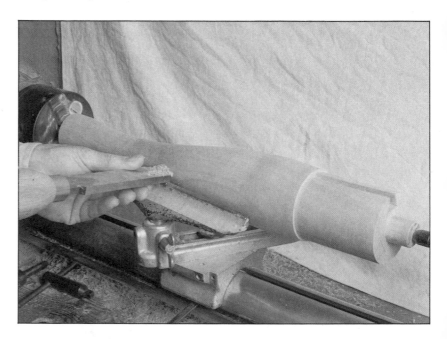

Fig 7 Rough turning the column shape

Make a card template to mark the dovetails on the bottom of the post base. Take care to position the template dead centre then temporarily secure with two pins before firmly marking the dovetail ends and vertical lines of the slots.

The joints can be chiselled out on the lathe, providing that light cuts are made. Remove the driving centre and substitute a three-jaw chuck which adds more stability to the column when cutting the joints. Before starting each joint ensure that both ends of the column are secure and that the chuck is held firmly in the required position. Using a firmer chisel cut the slot of the sliding dovetail to the required depth. Cut the angled walls next, Fig 8, and finally clean up the full length of the slot bottom with a paring chisel. When all three are done, leave the column on the lathe where it will be convenient for checking the leg joints for fit.

The next process can only be completed after the leg tenons have been made as described under Legs.

When the joint fitting has been completed, turn the spigot diameter to provide a firm fit with the brace. If a threaded spigot is preferred, turn to the required diameter and thread between centres as shown in Fig 11. The column body can now be finished off and sanded smooth.

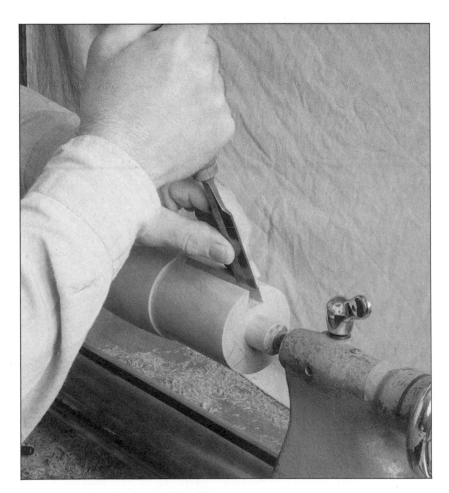

Fig 8 Cutting the angled wall of a sliding dovetail

Legs

Make a card template of the leg. Mark out each leg with the length running parallel to the direction of grain, see Fig 9. First cut the flat side which is to be jointed, then sand dead straight and square. Mark out the dovetails, then saw and carefully chisel out, periodically checking with the column joints until a smooth but firm sliding fit is achieved.

Fig 9 Marking out the legs

Cut the legs to shape, finish sand, then dry assemble to the column, making any necessary adjustments before gluing, see Fig 10.

Fitting the legs of the small stand is demanding. Great care is needed when cutting the curved face of the rounded upper edges which need to blend with the column side. A paring gauge, bevelled on the inside, is ideal for this purpose.

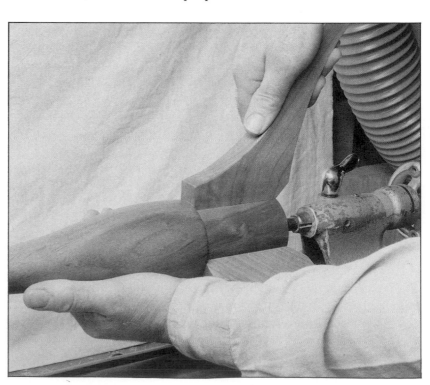

Fig 10 Dry assemble the legs with the column secured on the lathe

Baseplate

For the small stand, make a card template and mark out the baseplate, shown in dotted lines on the plan of base, Fig 6. Lightly centre pop the pin positions then drill through with a 1mm diameter bit. Cut out the shape with tin snips and file or grind the edges smooth. Using gimp pins, pin the plate to the column base and legs.

The column spigot can now be glued or screwed to the brace, taking care with the larger stand to position the length of the brace in line with one projecting leg.

Finishing

Two contrasting methods of finish have been used on these stands. The small example has been stained dark brown then given two coats of gloss varnish, rubbed down lightly with fine wire wool after each coat then wax polished to a high gloss.

For a more natural finish, apply boiled linseed oil, rub well in then leave to dry for several days before wax polishing to a fine lustre. ■

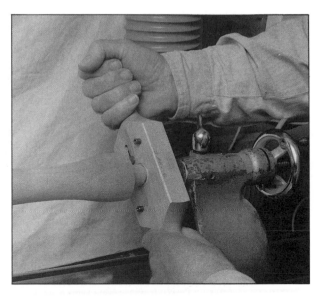

Fig 11 Threading the column spigot on the lathe

CUTTING LIST
Finished sizes in mm
Maple or Cherry

		Large Stand	Small Stand	
1	Top	505 dia.×19	400 dia.×12.5	*
1	Column	473×80 dia.	502×51 dia.	*
3	Legs	372×91×22	284×102×16	
1	Brace	349×127×19	178 dia.×19	
1	Baseplate	—	115 dia.×1	
4	Countersunk-head steel screws	32×8s	19×8s	
4	Gimp pins	—	12.5 long	

* The number of pieces used for the top will depend on the width of boards available. Add 2mm on to the thickness to allow for finishing.

* To allow for roughing out and finishing the post, add up to 20mm on the length and 10mm on the diameter.

Dining Chair

Long pine benches were the earliest form of dining room seating used by the Shakers. They were eventually replaced by individual chairs with low slat backs which gave an improvement in creature comfort that was greatly appreciated.
By being low enough to fit under the long trestle tables, a neat and tidy appearance could be maintained as well as making serving and clearing convenient.

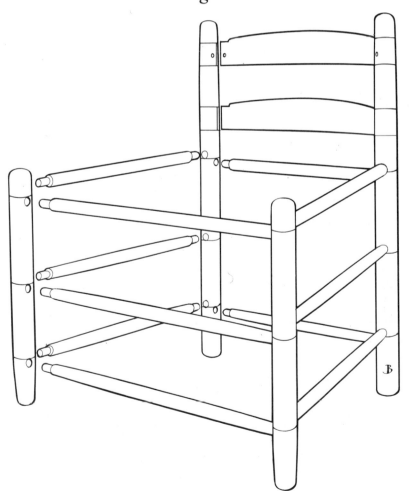

A LATER, MORE comfortable two-slat dining chair from Watervliet, New York, has a maple frame and splint seat. Although these were the most commonly used materials, I have reproduced this example in yew with a more durable fabric tape seating.

Most of the operations involved in making the dining chair are described in the more extensive Rocking Chair project. Refer to these in conjunction with the following instructions which are arranged in order of procedure.

Slats, mould and bending

Make the slats and mould first, see Figs 1 and 2. Soak the slats for approximately 1½ hours in near boiling water then leave to dry in the mould for seven or eight days at warm room temperature.

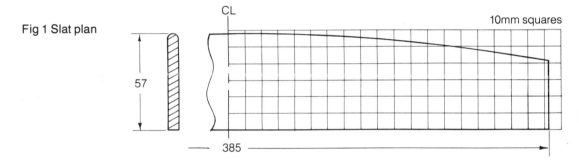

Fig 1 Slat plan

CL

10mm squares

57

385

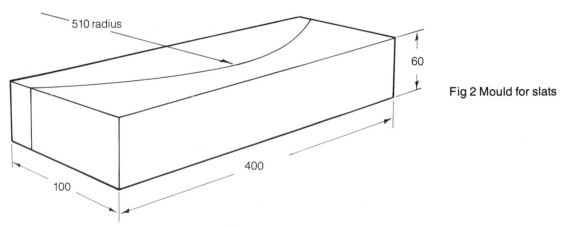

510 radius

60

Fig 2 Mould for slats

400

100

Turning

Turn the spindles and tenons as shown in Fig 3 – four straight seat rails and seven tapered rungs. Note that, unlike the rocker, all the tenon shoulders are chamfered.

Turn the posts straight and parallel then sand smooth to size ready for jointing.

Jointing

A 650mm-long jointing fixture, similar to the one used for the rocker, is required to support the posts when drilling the mortises.

Make a full-size drawing of the frame plan, Fig 4. All the mortise angles are taken from this plan, so accuracy is critical. Mark out the positions using the main assembly drawing, Fig 5. Mortises for the spindles are drilled 19mm deep with a 16mm flat bit and the 22mm deep slat mortises are initially drilled out with a 4mm diameter dowel bit.

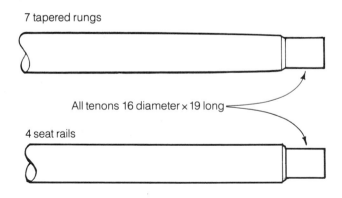

7 tapered rungs

All tenons 16 diameter × 19 long

4 seat rails

Fig 3 Spindles

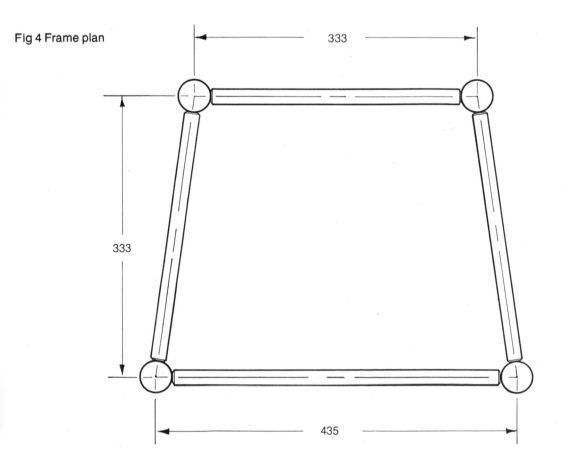

Fig 4 Frame plan

333

333

435

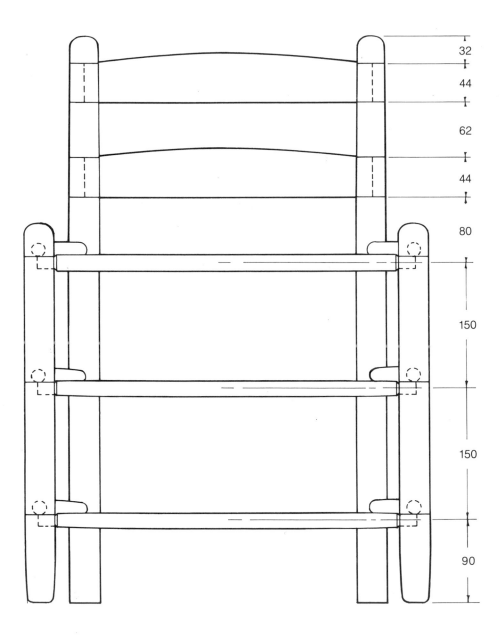

Fig 5 Main assembly

When jointing has been completed, finish shaping the posts on the lathe. After sanding smooth, cut the scroll marks with the skew chisel held on edge. Although these marks correspond with the mortise positions, I suspect that they were made for decoration and not for practical reasons. Leave the back posts on the lathe ready for fitting the slats.

Remove the dried slats from the mould and sand smooth. Leaving an equal amount of waste at both ends, mark off and cut to length, see mortise layout, Fig 6. Place each slat in position on the full-size

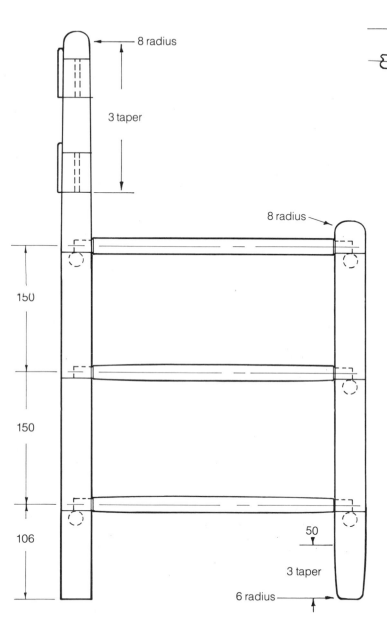

8 radius

3 taper

8 radius

Finished lengths of slats after bending

345

Fig 6 Mortise layout

150

150

106

50

3 taper

6 radius

frame plan and mark out the top shoulders of the tenons, remembering to allow for the taper in the post. Cut these carefully then check for fit, making any necessary adjustments.

Before parting the back posts off to length they will need to be shortened by 4mm at the base. This will cause a slight incline in the finished chair which conforms with the original example. I have purposely not mentioned this earlier to avoid confusion when marking out.

Assembly and finishing

Dry assemble the complete chair, checking in turn that each spindle tenon is not too tight, see Fig 7. When satisfied, glue the back frame using a sash cramp with padded jaws to nip up any obstinate joints.

The top slat/post joints are strengthened by 6mm diameter dowels 32mm long. Mark the centres and drill at the required angle to a depth of 30mm. Glue the dowels and tap home. Continuing with the assembly, glue the front frame complete with side rails and lower on to the back frame. Place the complete assembly on the full-size frame plan and nip up all the joints so that the feet correspond with the plan.

When the glue has set, sand the projecting dowel heads flush with the posts and clean up the completed assembly ready for finishing, see Fig 8. The choice of finish will depend on personal taste, but whether oil or varnish, sand smooth when dry then wax polish.

Fig 7 Checking the spindle tenons for fit during dry assembly

Seating

As with the rocker, two colours of tape have been used to weave the seat. Dark brown for the warp – front to back, and beige for the weft – side to side. A darker colour is chosen for the warp because the seat front has most wear and is more prone to being soiled.

The simple chequered weave adds the finishing touch to this sturdy little chair. Its uncomplicated design, which was originally for a specific purpose with comfort in mind, displays fundamental qualities so characteristically Shaker. ■

Pedestal tables

Canterbury step chest

Drop leaf table

Dining chair

Rocking chair

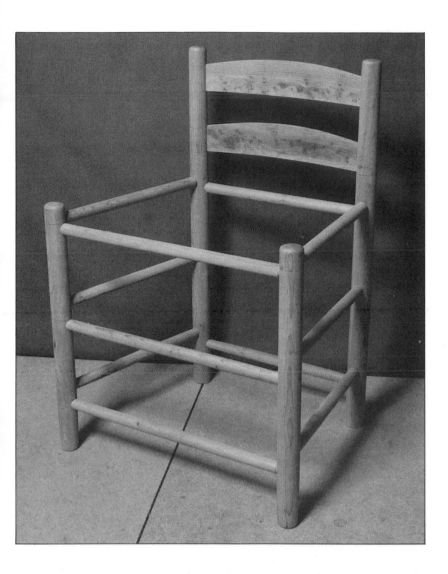

Fig 8 Completed chair, ready for
finishing before weaving the seat

CUTTING LIST
Finished sizes in mm

Cherry or Maple

		Length	Width	Thickness
2	Back posts	652	35 dia.	
2	Front posts	438	35 dia.	
2	Slats	385	55	6
3	Spindles: Front	438	19 dia.	
6	Side	341	19 dia.	
2	Back	337	19 dia.	

40mm of 6mm diameter dowelling

40mm has been included in the length of the slats to
allow for bending. The slats are initially prepared to 7mm
thickness, then sanded down after bending to fit the 6mm
wide post mortises.

All turned pieces are made from lengths of material
initially sawn square in section, approximately 4mm more
across the flats than the required finished diameter. Add
an extra 25mm on each length to allow for waste.

The 25mm wide tape used for weaving the seat will need
to be ordered before starting the project, see Sources and
Suppliers.

Rocking Chair

The first Shaker chairs were made at the New
Lebanon community, New York State in 1789.
For over 150 years production continued at
various levels until in 1942 Eldress Sarah
Collins, together with a small group of
surviving Shaker sisters,
assembled the last known
genuine examples.

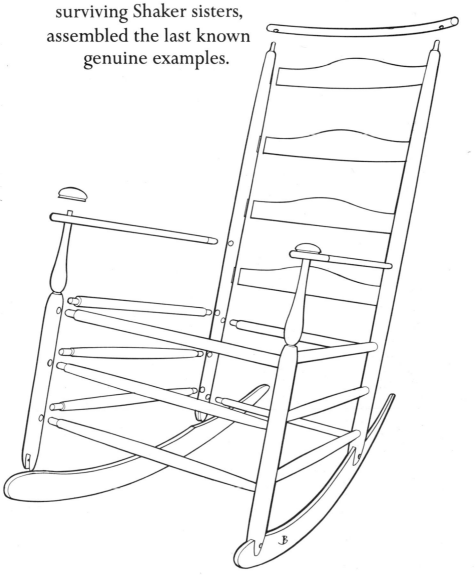

D URING THIS PERIOD the design of rocking chairs was developed and refined throughout most communities, and although the basic appearance remained unchanged the shapes of some parts were noticeably different.

The rocker shown here has been reproduced in birds' eye maple and is typical of those made at the New Lebanon workshops in the 1840s. By removing excess wood from the posts and spindles the chair is given a lightweight, delicate appearance and yet is remarkably strong. This strength has been further supplemented by weaving the seat with worsted tape.

Making the rocker involves several aspects of furniture making which should appeal to the more experienced woodturner. Equipped with a standard kit, taping the seat will provide an interesting diversion from the usual workshop practice.

Procedure

Most lathes are too short to accommodate the back posts, so a simple extension will need to be devised, see under Turning. This extension is used only to allow the shaping of the post ends. Because of the difficulties which would be found when turning the full length between centres, I advise using the rotary plane method as a safer, more efficient alternative. Described more fully under Rotary Planes, these tools are easy to use and can quickly produce long lengths of dowellng with an excellent finish.

Throughout the project a full-size drawing of the frame plan is used for marking out and checking the sizes of various pieces, so this will need to be drawn accurately.

The back slats and shawl rail are left in their moulds for several days after being soaked. Make these immediately after the moulds so that while they are drying to shape, work can be continued on other pieces.

Moulds and bending

Using scrapwood, saw out the two moulds needed for bending the slats and shawl rail, see Fig 1. Mark off each curve then very carefully bandsaw to the line. If there are any high spots on the curved surfaces, remove with sandpaper.

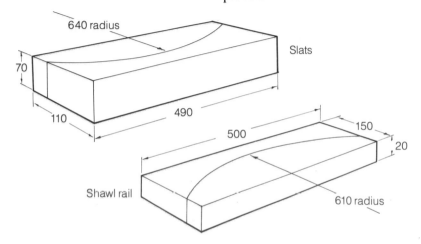

Fig 1 Moulds

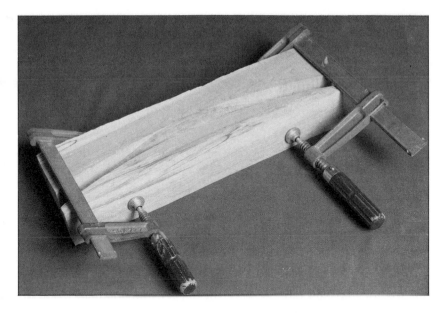

Fig 2 Cramp up the slats while still hot

When the slats and shawl rail have been made – see under the relevant headings – immerse them in a bath of near boiling water which is kept simmering. Cover the bath with a metal tray or board and leave to soak. 1½ hours should be sufficient for the slats and 2½ hours for the rail.

Transfer from bath to mould as quickly as possible so that the pieces are still hot when being tightened, see Fig 2. The time required for drying is determined by temperature. Preferring not to accelerate this process, I found that seven or eight days in a warm room was adequate. When the dried pieces are taken from the moulds they will spring back approximately 20 per cent to the required shape. Put them to one side ready for fitting later, see under Jointing.

Slats, arms and rockers

Using the three scale drawings as a guide, see Fig 3, make card templates. Mark out each piece, cut to shape and sand all sides smooth. Make the slats first, ready to soak for bending.

Continue with the arms as follows. Mark out the rounded tenons and file to shape, cleaning up the shoulders with a chisel. Leave a little extra on the diameters to allow for adjustments when fitting to the back post mortises. Before marking the centre for the front post spigot hole, check the template for accuracy against the frame plan. If the centres correspond when the tenon shoulder is up to the back post, proceed to mark this centre on each arm then drill through with a 12mm bit. The front and side edges can now be shaped and sanded smooth, see Fig 4.

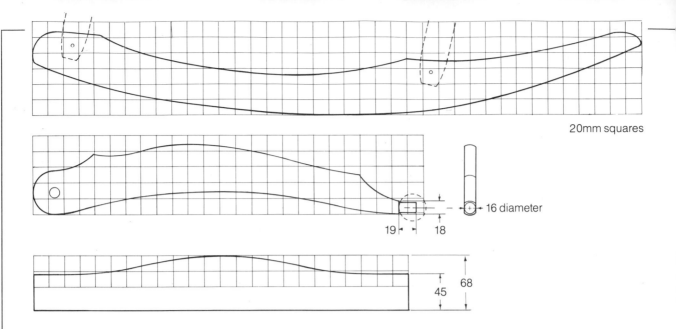

20mm squares

16 diameter

19 18

68

45

Fig 3 Rocker, arms and slat plans

Rotary planes

Ironically I was first introduced to the English-made rotary planes by my American friend John Wilson, the Shaker oval box maker. These tools included a 'rounder', which converts square sectioned timber into dowelling, and an optional 'trap', which cuts tapers and curves on the dowelling.

The 35mm rounder required for the posts will cost about the same as a threadcutting box of similar size. Although not essential, considerable time could be saved by using this method to shape the spindle bodies. Unfortunately a separate rounder is needed for each diameter of spindle and the total expense would be difficult to justify unless larger quantities were required.

The suppliers, who are also the sole manufacturers, provide full instructions with each tool, see Sources and Suppliers.

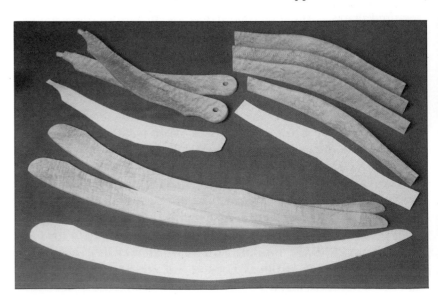

Fig 4 Completed slats, arms and rockers with templates

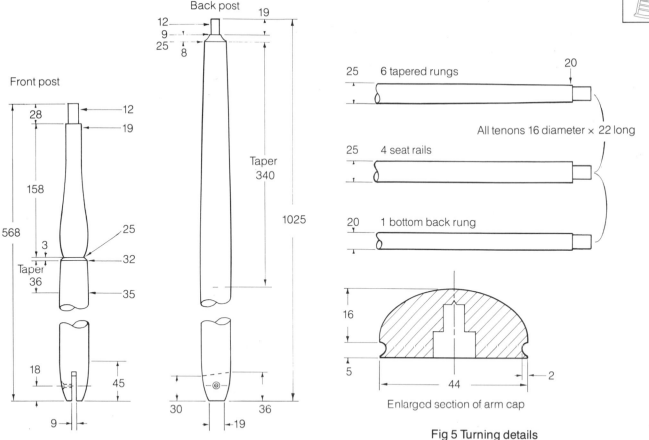

Front post

Back post

158

568

28 — 12
— 19

25
3
Taper
36
18
35
45
9

12
9
25
8
19

Taper
340

1025

30   36
19

25   6 tapered rungs   20

All tenons 16 diameter × 22 long

25   4 seat rails

20   1 bottom back rung

16

5

44   2

Enlarged section of arm cap

Fig 5 Turning details

Turning

Centre both ends of all the pieces of material which have been prepared for the posts, shawl rail and spindles. Starting with the shawl rail, turn the full length between centres using a roughing gouge. Next, carefully smooth down with a skew chisel, checking that the sides are flat and parallel before sanding to finished size. The rail can now be soaked, together with the back slats, ready for bending.

Spindles

Turn all the spindles as described for the shawl rail, but before finish sanding mark off each length, allowing for an equal amount of waste at both ends. Five spindles have parallel sides – four seat rails and the thinner bottom back rail, see Fig 5. Mark the tenon positions and turn to size providing a firm fit in the post mortises. To ensure consistent accuracy check each tenon with a pre-drilled piece of scrapwood. Finish sand then slightly dull the edges of each shoulder before parting off to length.

The six remaining spindles are taper turned, see Fig 6. Only partly cut the tenons before turning the tapers – these are completed after the tapered spindle body has been sanded smooth.

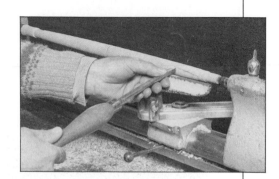

Fig 6 Turn the tapered spindles between centres, starting with a roughing gouge

Arm caps

The arm caps are shaped on a screw chuck, see enlarged section of end cap, Fig 5. Mark out the circular base and drill the spigot hole 12mm deep with a flat bit. On the same centre, drill a hole for the chuck screw, taking care not to exceed a total depth of 18mm. A thin ply or hardboard spacing disc is placed between the cap and chuck to give clearance when cutting the side grooves. Shape the caps and sand to a fine finish.

Posts

Chamfer the corners of the prepared timber to fit the larger end of the rounder. Round down all four lengths, see Fig 7, then finish sand the two shorter posts on the lathe.

To accommodate the back posts, most lathes will need to be extended. This can be done quite easily by making an additional support for the tailstock. Two pieces of scrapwood were used to extend the round bedded lathe shown in Fig 8. To duplicate the shape of the bed, one piece has been turned between centres with a spigot cut on one end to fit tightly inside the bed end. A flat, cut along the rounded underside, locates on a wide spacing block. A vertical hole is drilled through the two pieces and counterbored to accommodate a long bolt. The bolt is fed through both pieces and the existing bolt hole in the tailstock base then tightened up. With the assembly in position, so that the headstock and tailstock centres correspond, clamp or bolt the spacing block to the lathe bench. (For clarity the clamps are not shown in the photograph.) A similar device could be adapted to suit most lathe bed designs.

Fig 7 Using the rotary plane rounding tool to round down the posts

If the bench does not extend beyond the tailstock end of the lathe, a simple plywood or chipboard box-type floor unit could be fabricated and clamped to the bench end.

Sand the back posts smooth on the lathe ready for jointing. All the post mortises must be completed next before continuing with this section – see Jointing.

Fig 8 The simple tailstock extension for a round bed lathe. Note the top spigot detail of the back post

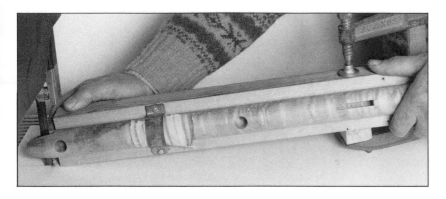

Fig 9 Bandsawing the rocker slots

When the slats have been checked for fit and adjusted to satisfaction, continue to shape the posts on the lathe. After shaping, sand to a fine finish before turning the spigots. Take particular care with these diameters to ensure a comfortable push-fit with the respective shawl rail and hand cap joints. Saw off the waste at both ends then mark off the rocker joints at the base of each post.

I have cut these joints on the bandsaw with the posts held in the jointing fixture, see Fig 9. A piece of flat board has been clamped to the bandsaw table to extend the working surface. The post is positioned so that when the fixture is laid flat, the slot to be cut is in the same vertical line as the side spindle mortises. Tilt the fixture and set to the required angle using a spacing block and clamp. The joints can now be cut with controlled accuracy. Finally, clean up the top of each slot with a chisel.

Drill and countersink the holes for the rocker securing screws. These are drilled only half way through the posts from the outer side.

Jointing

A jointing fixture is required to support the posts when drilling the mortises, see Fig 10. This consists of two accurately prepared 1 metre lengths of softwood, 20×40mm and 20×20mm, which are glued and screwed together to form a cradle. Two sheet-metal brackets –

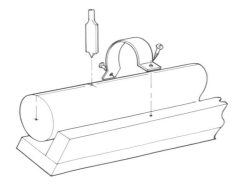

Fig 10 Jointing fixture

Fig 11 Drilling the mortises with the drill bed tilted at 45°

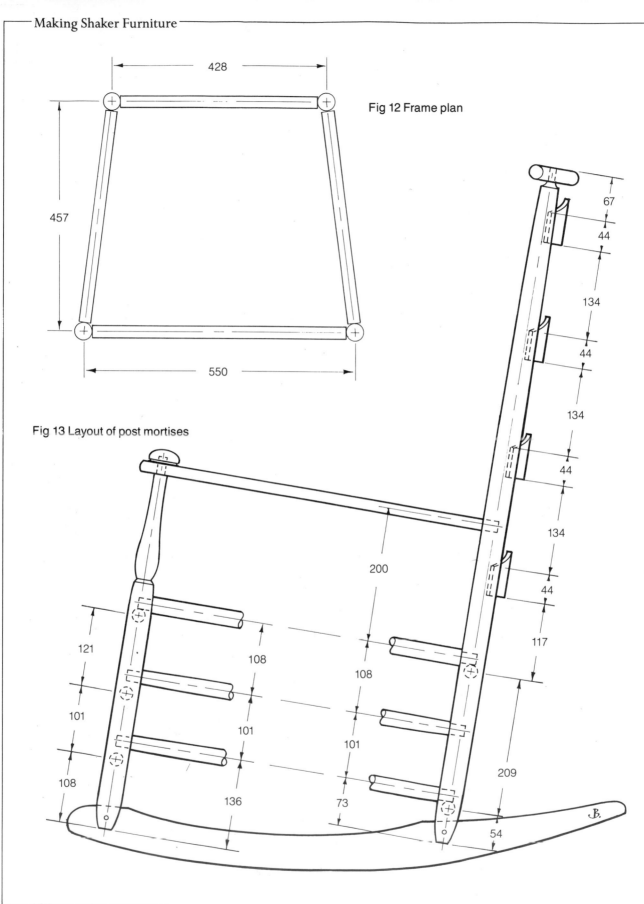

428

457

550

Fig 12 Frame plan

Fig 13 Layout of post mortises

67
44
134
44
134
44
134
44
117

200
108
108
101
101
209
73
54

121
101
108
136

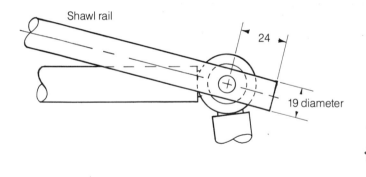

Shawl rail

24

19 diameter

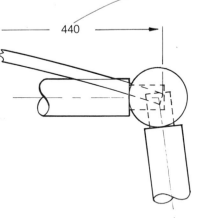

Finished length of slats after bending

440

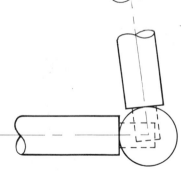

Fig 14 Mortise details

shaped, drilled and screwed to the cradle – hold the posts in position. To prevent the brackets from marking the posts, insert a piece of cloth or leather between the two before tightening up.

Tilt the drill bed to 45° and clamp a straightedged board to it. The board serves as a horizontal fence and its position must be set precisely so that when each mortise is drilled vertically, the mortise and drill bit centres correspond exactly (Fig 11).

The following operations are critical and their success depends on the accuracy of the full-size drawing of the frame plan, Fig 12.

With the end of each post held firmly in position on the plan, mark out the centre line of each row of mortises. These centre lines can be accurately extended along the length of the post sides by using the top sides of the fixture as a straightedge. To avoid confusion, mark an identity letter at the bottom of the posts next to each centre line. Allowing an equal amount for waste at each end, mark out the post lengths and spindle joint positions, see Fig 13.

Using a 16mm flat bit, drill all the spindle mortises 22mm deep, see Fig 14. The arm mortises share the same centre line as the side spindles. Mark their centres and drill 19mm deep. Return to the frame plan with the back posts and mark out the slat mortise centre lines, then the positions. Using a 4mm dowel bit, drill out the bulk of the waste to a depth of 22mm. Transfer the jointing fixture complete with post to a bench and clean up the mortises with a chisel to the finished size of 6mm wide × 44mm long. Alternatively this operation could be done with the posts between centres on the lathe.

The slats and shawl rail can be finished off at this stage. Sand all surfaces smooth and cut to the finished lengths, see Fig 14. The two post spigot holes will need to be drilled through the shawl rail very carefully to avoid splintering the undersides when breaking through.

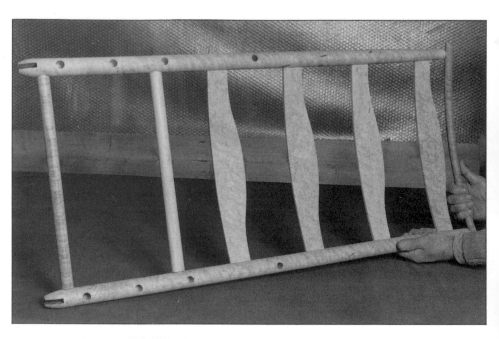

Fig 15 Assemble the back frame first

Assembly and finishing

Dry assemble the complete rocker starting with the back frame, see Fig 15. The front frame is next, then lowered complete with side rails and arm rests on to the back frame. Push all the joints well home before fitting the rockers and hand caps (see Fig 16 – hand caps omitted). Bradawl the rockers through the countersunk holes at the bottom outer side of each post, then drive in the screws. Repeat this procedure when finally gluing, but also have a sash cramp with padded jaws ready to nip up any obstinate joints. The bottom rockers are not glued, thus allowing replacement if necessary.

When the glue has dried, round off the projecting post spigots on the shawl rail and lightly clean up the complete assembly with fine sandpaper. After dusting off, apply either a varnished or oiled finish, whichever is preferred.

Fig 16 Dry assembly of rocker without arm caps

Seating

The Shakers wove their earlier seats with a narrow hickory splint or straw rush. After the 1850s these materials were replaced by a more practical worsted tape. This was homemade in a variety of colours and proved to be not only more durable and comfortable but easier and quicker to weave.

A very similar tape is still being produced in a wide range of colours and is available by the roll or in kit form, both including weaving instructions (see Sources and Suppliers).

The seat is woven in two directions: first, the warp – front to back, then the weft – side to side. A 19mm thick foam rubber pad is slid between the upper and lower layers of the warp before starting the weft weave. The spacer pad maintains contact with the two layers so that any weight on the top is shared by both. This prevents sagging and reduces wear.

Weaving the seat is not difficult. The main requirement, even for a beginner, is patience – this was my first chair.

Seeing the completed rocker on the workshop floor for the first time was a magical moment. With a slight touch on the arm, the smooth motion forwards and backwards made it seem as though it had a life of its own. ■

CUTTING LIST
Finished sizes in mm
Maple

		Length	Width	Thickness
4	Slats	480	68	6
1	Shawl rail	520	19 dia.	
2	Back posts	1025	35 dia.	
2	Front posts	568	35 dia.	
3	Spindles: Front	559	25 dia.	
6	Sides	470	25 dia.	
1	Back	439	25 dia.	
1	Bottom back	439	20 dia.	
2	Arms	493	89	16
2	Hand caps		45 dia.	20
2	Rockers	780	105	9
4	25mm Number 8 Countersunk-head steel screws			

40mm has been included in the length of the shawl rail and slats to allow for bending. The slats are initially prepared to 7mm thickness then sanded down after bending to fit the 6mm wide post mortises.

All turned pieces other than the hand caps are made from lengths of material initially sawn square in section, approximately 4mm more across flats than the required finished diameter. Add an extra 25mm on each length to allow for waste.

Sources and Suppliers

Tape seating kits   Shaker Workshops
PO Box 1028
Concord
MA 01742
USA

UK Representatives:
The Shaker Shop Ltd
27 Harcourt Street
London   W1H 1DT

Copper tacks   John Wilson
The Home Shop
500 East Broadway Highway
Charlotte
Michigan 48813
USA

Rotary planes,
rounders and traps   Ashem Crafts
2 Oakleigh Avenue
Hallow
Worcester   WR2 6NG

Bibliography

John Kassay, *The Book of Shaker Furniture*, University of Massachusetts Press, 1980
Charles R. Muller and Timothy Rieman, *The Shaker Chair*, Canal Press, 1984
Edward D. Andrews and Faith Andrews, *Shaker Furniture, The Craftsmanship of an American Communal Sect*, Dover Publications, 1964
Robert F. W. Meader, *Illustrated Guide to Shaker Furniture*, Dover Publications, 1972
June Sprigg and David Larkin, *Shaker Life, Work and Art*, Cassell, 1987
June Sprigg, *Shaker Design*, Whitney Norton, 1986

Metric Conversion Table

1/4″	—	6mm	6″	—	150mm	26″	—	660mm
3/8″	—	10mm	6 1/8″	—	155mm	27″	—	685mm
1/2″	—	13mm	6 1/4″	—	160mm	28″	—	710mm
5/8″	—	16mm	6 1/2″	—	165mm	29″	—	735mm
3/4″	—	19mm	6 3/4″	—	170mm	30″	—	760mm
7/8″	—	22mm	7″	—	178mm	31″	—	785mm
1″	—	25mm	7 1/8″	—	181mm	32″	—	815mm
1 1/8″	—	30mm	7 1/4″	—	185mm	33″	—	840mm
1 1/4″	—	32mm	7 1/2″	—	190mm	34″	—	865mm
1 3/8″	—	35mm	7 3/4″	—	195mm	35″	—	890mm
1 1/2″	—	38mm	8″	—	200mm	36″	—	915mm
1 5/8″	—	40mm	8 1/4″	—	210mm	37″	—	940mm
1 3/4″	—	45mm	8 1/2″	—	215mm	38″	—	965mm
2″	—	50mm	8 3/4″	—	220mm	39″	—	990mm
2 1/8″-2 1/4″	—	55mm	9″	—	230mm	40″	—	1015mm
2 3/8″	—	60mm	9 1/4″	—	235mm	41″	—	1040mm
2 1/2″	—	63mm	9 1/2″	—	240mm	42″	—	1065mm
2 5/8″	—	65mm	9 3/4″	—	250mm	43″	—	1090mm
2 3/4″	—	70mm	10″	—	255mm	44″	—	1120mm
3″	—	75mm	10 1/8″	—	257mm	45″	—	1145mm
3 1/8″	—	80mm	11″	—	280mm	46″	—	1170mm
3 1/4″	—	83mm	12″	—	305mm	47″	—	1195mm
3 1/2″		88mm	13″	—	330mm	48″	—	1220mm
3 2/3″	—	93mm	14″	—	355mm	49″	—	1245mm
3 3/4″	—	95mm	15″	—	380mm	50″	—	1270mm
4″	—	100mm	16″	—	405mm	51″	—	1295mm
4 1/8″	—	105mm	17″	—	430mm	52″	—	1320mm
4 1/4″-4 3/8″	—	110mm	18″	—	460mm	53″	—	1345mm
4 1/2″	—	115mm	19″	—	485mm	54″	—	1370mm
4 3/4″	—	120mm	20″	—	510mm	55″	—	1395mm
5″	—	125mm	21″	—	535mm	56″	—	1420mm
5 1/8″	—	130mm	22″	—	560mm	57″	—	1450mm
5 1/4″	—	133mm	23″	—	585mm	58″	—	1475mm
5 1/2″	—	140mm	24″	—	610mm	59″	—	1500mm
5 3/4″	—	145mm	25″	—	635mm	60″	—	1525mm

To obtain the metric size for dimensions under 60″, not shown in the above table, multiply the imperial size in inches by 25·4 and round to the nearest millimetre taking 0·5 mm upwards.

e.g. 9 1/8 × 25·4 = 231·8
= 232 mm

To obtain the metric size for dimensions over 60″ multiply the imperial size in inches by 25·4 and round up to the nearest 10 mm taking 5 mm upwards.

e.g. 67″ × 25·4 = 1701·8
= 1700 mm

Other titles available from GMC Publications Ltd:

Woodworking Plans and Projects
40 More Woodworking Plans and Projects
Woodworking Crafts Annual
Sharpening and Care of Woodworking Tools and Equipment   John Sainsbury
Turning Miniatures in Wood   John Sainsbury
Woodcarving: A Complete Course   Ron Butterfield
Pleasure and Profit from Woodturning   Reg Sherwin
Creating a Miniature World   Patricia King
Making Unusual Miniatures   Graham Spalding
Furniture Projects for the Home   Ernest Parrott
Seat Weaving   Ricky Holdstock
Green Woodwork   Mike Abbott
The Incredible Router   Jeremy Broun
Woodturning: A Foundation Course   Keith Rowley
Upholstery: A Complete Course   David James
How to Make Tudor Dolls' Houses   Derek Rowbottom
Care and Repair   5th edition of the essential handbook
Directory of Members of the Guild of Master Craftsmen 1989–90

All these books may be ordered by post from the publishers at
Castle Place, 166 High Street, Lewes, East Sussex BN7 1XU, telephone 0273
477374. Please write or phone for further details. Credit card orders are accepted.